FROM RAT CATCHER TO COMMODORE

by

Rosalie Langan

Contents

MARK JOSEPH HIGGINS

Welcome on board the lifetime voyage of a remarkable gentleman who, from being a rat catcher on his Uncle Gemmy's farm in County Wexford, became Commodore of the Fleet of Reardon Smith Shipping Company. He was awarded an M.B.E. He lived for 103 years.

His natural way of treating everyone with courtesy and kindness endeared him to all who had the privilege to meet him.

Sit back and enjoy this great voyage in his own words. All the stories Mark tells are his own recollections as he looked back over a very long life.

For your information, I was born in Waterford on 6th March 1918. It was a momentous occasion when I arrived on the scene. We moved to Wexford in later years and, unfortunately, my parents had to bring me with them! I was four years old when we first arrived there. It was 1922. It was my mother's hometown.

I was one of six children. Three boys and three girls. Well balanced. I was the youngest. Three died young. My sister Patty and brothers Jim and Teddy all died of tuberculosis. The remaining brood all managed to live to old age. Agnes was 87 when she died and Maureen just on 100. I am still a young fella at 103!

In Wexford, my father bought a new house, 10 Thomas Street. Father insisted there was a flush toilet. It cost him a lot of money but he was proud of having that installed. He bought an extra plot land at end of Thomas Street where, in subsequent years, father housed his car. Mother had a trap there.

ROYAL IRISH CONSTABULARY

My father was in the Royal Irish Constabulary. He was a Sergeant when he retired and got a pension from them. They were a highly trained force. The R.I.C. was the British Police and the natives did not like the English cops. It stands to reason. That was the change-over. They were getting out of Ireland. That was the end of English rule.

We got the GARDA then. Strange to say, my father got a very good executive job with the GARDA in Dublin. He was in charge of a Department. Remember he would have had to live in Dublin and my mother was not on for that. She did not want to live in Dublin so that was the end of the Police Force.

It was a tough time getting a job, but he ended up working for the Income Tax in Wexford and remained there until he retired. They thought very highly of him. He was very literate was my old man. Beautiful handwriting. You could read every word he wrote. You cannot say that for me. That is the reason I got myself a typewriter.

ROSSLARE

Each summer all the family went by horse and trap to Rosslare for two months, the whole of the school holidays. Mother used to rent a bungalow. Father came weekends. He went back Monday morning early on.

We also had a bathing box on the beach. Father built that box in our back yard in Wexford. He numbered every bolt and screw when it was ready for use and time to take it to Rosslare. Then he dismantled the box and hired a truck and himself and my brothers took it to Rosslare. We had already prepared a site for it, which we rented.

You would get changed in it to go swimming. It had a primus stove, two folding beds, two folding tables and two chairs. I thank my parents for that to this very day because in those days people did not have holidays.

BRIDE STREET CHURCH

Mother was a very holy woman. She went to 7 a.m. Mass every morning of her life. God be good to her. Any chance she got, out came the rosary. We had to be in at 7 p.m. for the evening rosary. We did not mind the rosary, it was all the trimmings. I was an altar boy all the years I lived in Wexford. I got up at 6 a.m. on many a cold winter's morning to ring the bell for people to attend 7 a.m. Mass.

Sister Gerard looked after the altar boys. A lovely nun, God be good to her. She was always telling us off for being so noisy, warning us all the time not to get our vestments dirty. We dripped in lace. Red cape with Sacred Heart on left hand side. They were lovely things. We looked like mini-Cardinals. The Pope would have been jealous of us. We were forever getting into trouble playing football in the satin shoes.

We knew every word of the Latin Mass. At Benediction I swung the thurible. Our ambition was to raise as much smoke as we could. The idea was to make everybody sneeze! Mother Superior would have killed us if she could. The nuns filed out of the convent in pairs, all dressed in white with veils over their faces. I used to think they looked like ghosts. We were not a bit afraid of them. I called her Gerry to her face and do you know what, she liked it. The nuns were fond of us.

Once a year in the Convent they gave us servers a real good feast. Boy that was something. The tables were laden with confectionary which we never saw in our lives. We were given bags of goodies to take home and everyone would be waiting for them to arrive. They played games with us, and they liked to play rough. We would be sitting on chairs and you me and the nun would be running for the empty chair and she would give us the shoulder ha! They were nice people. We used to get on very well with them.

Once upon a time there were around thirty of them attached to the church. They were a very high Order. For some it could be a tough life. Rich men's daughters went in. A lot were let down by love but there were a lot of vocations. They were always praying. Getting up in the middle of the night to say prayers. A lot are happy, but I would not be.

They attended the ordinary services, Mass and all the rest of it. When they attended Mass, they always came out veiled. You never saw their faces. They went to their special pews which were on the altar. Mother Superior would be there. She controlled them. They knelt- down together. When Mass ended, they went straight from the main altar into their quarters. They had a beautiful garden. In the garden was a cemetery. They were buried in their own grounds. It will still be there. Some people will look after it. Now there are no nuns there. Young girls will not go into that.

GLASNEVIN CEMETRY

Go to Glasnevin, Ireland's National Cemetery in Dublin to read the inscriptions.

The Book of Kells in Dublin was written by the Monks hundreds and hundreds of years ago. Beautifully illuminated. I suppose it would take a long time to do one page.

CHRISTIAN BROTHERS' SCHOOL

First school was Sisters of Mercy. Then Christian Brothers School, George Street. If your parents could afford it you went to the College. You went to the college usually if you had the Priesthood in mind.

We could not afford the College. Very few could afford it. We had a good basic education, but it was beaten into us with a leather strap. They were hard men. I was never much of a scholar and did not enjoy my school years very much. I had a fair grasp of maths, geometry and was well versed in geography, history, and a good grasp of algebra. I thank them for that.

I was able to get out and do the things I did eventually purely because of my education and my parent's upbringing. I left aged 15 without any certificates but I was prepared for the world. I went to sea shortly afterwards aged fifteen and a half.

We had good parents who looked after us very well and those were the days when hunger was prevalent. Food was very, very scarce. I must say I never experienced anything like that. I went to school with many associates in their bare feet, winter, and summer. You look around you now and how many do you see in their bare feet? Imagine having to get up and go out to school in your bare feet. It was rough times and unless your parents were very conscientious children could suffer. If your parent drank, for instance, you went without something, you know. The money that should have been spent for food to eat was spent on drink and the family suffered.

You never had a few shillings in the Bank. Any money you had you lived on it. Tuberculosis was very prevalent. I think I survived by being at sea. We owe a lot to our doctors who studied medicine and the National Health Service, of course.

Now, you take the telephone for granted. If you wanted to make a telephone call you had to go the Post Office. We had one telephone in Wexford town and that was only used for emergencies.

Even now the poorest have some sort of education.

Times have changed so much now that you would not recognise those times.

School days were ok. The usual young fellas gatching about. My first bicycle was a girl's bicycle. The bike's handlebars did not correspond with the wheels. The tyres were patched all over.

I was the youngest member of the gymnastic class. Teddy and Jim were also in the class. It was run by a fellow named Quinlan. He was a great big fella. My being the youngest and smallest always got the high jobs in the tableau and things like that. I was not too happy with it at the time but stayed with it. I broke my nose whilst in the gymnastic class. There was never anything done about it and it is still broken. On the whole I enjoyed my time in the gymnastic class.

RAT CATCHER UNCLE GEMMY'S FARM

Life was very enjoyable going out to Uncle Gemmy's farm where we worked all day, especially enjoyed harvest time. I got a few coppers for catching rats. I devised my own cardboard box and sat patiently waiting for them to come into my trap. I made a fair amount doing that as there were lots of rats on the farm.

Grandfather's family were cattle buyers in a big way. They had three butcher's shops in Wexford. They also had a slaughterhouse. They shipped cattle to an abattoir in Birkenhead. I grew up working and living often on Uncle Gemmy O'Rourke's farm in Gregorystown. My mother's family, the O'Rourkes, had three farms; Ballymorris, Gregorystown and White Mill.

When he bought cattle at a cattle fair it was my job to drive the cattle to Wexford harbour for shipment to England. Sometimes it would take a day. It was essential you had a dog to help you. The dog used to bite the ankles of the cows. They tried to retaliate by butting him, but they never did catch him. It was good really, even though unpaid labour.

I used to like a day when I started out early on a summer's morning with the old horse and cart. I was very keen on sport in those days, and I didn't ride the cart but dog trotted most of the way to Ballymorris. It was two and a half miles. Out to Gregorystown it was getting on for six miles. I thought nothing of it.

The O'Rourkes had a slaughterhouse. When they killed the cattle, grandmother (God be good to her) used to make black puddings and tripe and I used to give her a hand. There were buckets of blood all over the place. Bullock's blood of course. You had to stir it with your hands. You would be up to your shoulder in blood, stirring this thing up but we thought nothing of it. When we milked the cows, they flicked their tails full of dung into the bucket. It was drunk, dung and all. It was all part of life in those days. Nobody seemed to get ill or have bad tummies or come down with some of the diseases that are so prevalent now.

Gemmy went around all the Fairs in Wexford, and when I was not in school, he would take me with him. That was a great time. The earliest means of transport we had in those days was the old Tin Lizzy, the old Ford car with the canvas top and all that kind of stuff but I really enjoyed it.

The cattle Fairs were great experiences. The goings on. The fellas making bargains. The spitting in one another's hands and the arguing trying to seal the bargains. It was a great atmosphere. They always ended up in the local pubs. Everyone used to get very merry. I, of course, used to get a bottle of lemonade and a packet of biscuits. I thought it was great.

You know our expectations in those days weren't an awful lot. We were satisfied with little things and enjoyed it. I saw quite a lot of the county of Wexford going around the Fairs. Life was enjoyable. We played around the College field. A fella by the name Lucking and I had a swing up there. We had a fine time. I really enjoyed it.

I was expected to take over the farm but did not Gemmy up and marry and produce a son and a daughter? So, I was out in the cold.

My only future was doing messages for Uncle Gemmy. I was not too enamoured with that. I was left with no option but find another job. It was a stroke of luck because then I had to stand on my own two feet.

AUNT ANNIE'S HUSBAND CLASSICAL PIANIST IN OLD FARMHOUSE

My sister Maureen and I were going by bus to Wicklow, Dinard, close to Dunlavin, to visit Aunt Annie, a relation on my father's side. A neighbour of Maureen was on his way to Dublin and said he would drive us. The farmhouse was a long low building, one storey, with a thatched roof. Usual scruffiness of a farmhouse. Music coming from the farmhouse greeted us.

Maureen and I were surprised to see this character sitting in the kitchen at a grand piano playing classical music. Hens and chickens were his only audience. One or two were perched on the cross rail. Larry Maguire was his name.

It was reputed he had played with some famous Orchestra in London. He didn't go in for jazz or anything like that. He certainly looked the part. He had long hair curled up at the bottom. Larry played the piano all the time. That was the only thing he did. He didn't do any farm work. Aunt Annie said that is left to me.

Maureen and I coming home on the bus to Wexford were speculating how this character and Aunty Annie, an old woman farmer living there on her own, had ever got together. We never really got the answer to that one and even when I was talking to my father about it, he said he hadn't a clue either. So, you can make the best of that story.

So that's that. Now I will go on to the next tale.

CALL OF THE SEA

Now to continue my life story such as it is. I realised there wasn't much future in Wexford. The local papers at the time carried advertisements from British shipowners looking for people to go to sea, both as able seamen and cadets and so forth. A few of us mulled over this idea and Brendan Kelly of Whitemills was interested in going and Ginger Kirwan of Ballinagee. Also Brendan Corish. We all took part in the discussions.

I applied to various Shipping Companies with a view to being indentured. I finally got accepted and joined Sir William Reardon Smith & Sons of Cardiff in November 1939. Pay as an apprentice was the magnificent amount of sixty pounds for the whole four years. You had a roof over your head and you were fed and I still managed to send money home. We were a hell of a lot better off than some people. As long as you think you are well off that is the main thing.

The food on the ship left a lot to be desired. Our main staple food was porridge. It was the main food in prisons. I never broke the law, do not get that idea – well nobody found me out! Mind you to this day I still like my porridge.

I finished my four years apprenticeship and studied for my certificates and progressively acquired all three. I became Chief Officer and eventually for twenty- five years went as Captain. I am now thirty- six years retired and receiving my full pension, which gives me great satisfaction.

Laughing and singing,
Sweet Vale of Avoca! How calm could I rest
In Thy bosom of shade, with the friends I love best,
Where the storms that we feel in this cold world should cease
And our hearts, like these waters, be mingled in peace
And our hearts, like these waters, be mingled in peace

FIRST SHIP QUEEN CITY 1934-1939, £60 FOUR YEARS WORK

There was a great to do about getting things ready for the off. Sammy Gaul the local tailor in Wexford made the first uniform I ever possessed, and I was as proud as punch of that.

My mother, God be good to her, only left Wexford the once to go with me to join the ship in Cardiff, which was unusual to say the least because she wasn't a good traveller. She never liked to go far from home. We went from Rosslare Harbour to Fishguard, eventually arriving in Cardiff in the early hours of the morning. She couldn't understand the language. To come to Cardiff, which was a modern city, from her humble home in the hick town of Wexford was a big experience for her. I made up for it. She raised a son who roamed the world.

Cardiff in those days had a black and coloured population and neither mother nor myself had ever seen a black person before. She had to do some shopping for me. She had to buy a mattress consisting of a piece of calico filled with straw. We used to call them donkey breakfasts because I suppose a donkey would enjoy eating them. They needed replacing when they turned to dust. Mother got the mattress onto the bunk and made it up. That was the first and last time it was made for four years. In those days, the ship owners did not supply bedding of any description. You supplied your own. She also bought oil skins, sea boots and other odds and sods.

The Shipping Company demanded a surety of ten pounds, which was a lot of money in those days. I don't suppose mother had it to spare. She managed to persuade Uncle Gemmy to part with ten pounds and she had to pay him back in due course, which she did.

Eventually the great moment arrived when we took a taxi down to the docks to join the Queen City. She was in dry dock at the time. I was absolutely stunned, and so was mother, at the size of this monster sat in dry dock. She was about 7,000 tons. I was very much impressed by all the going on. She was being scraped and painted and so forth. We went on board and looked around to see who we could approach. Eventually a distinguished looking fellow in a white boiler suit approached us and said he was the Chief Officer of the ship. He was an elderly man. He was Welsh and went by the name Dai James. I subsequently got to know him. He was a nice fella. He took me to where the Apprentice Cadets lived. This was a room amidships. It could accommodate eight but there were usually six Apprentices at any one time.

He took me to this room and we were amazed at how six people could live in a place so small. There were six bunks and he pointed out the one nearest the door and said, "That is the only one that is not occupied. The rest of them are booked you will have to take that one." After being at sea for a few months I realised why nobody else wanted that bunk. If there was bad weather at all you damn well near got the sea in your bunk. But enough of that.

A HOLY WATER GOODBYE FROM MOTHER

When it was time for mother to go, I got permission from the Chief Officer to take her back up to the station at Cardiff. She could not wait to get back to Wexford. The train didn't go until 7 p.m. but we were there at 4 p.m. We were too terrified to go far from the station. I put her on the train at 7 o' clock. It was a very emotional thing to see your mother going off and leaving you. She was very upset and so was I. Anyway, off she went after drowning me with holy water and the rest of it and I went back to the ship but I felt very lonely that night. It was another eighteen months before I saw her again.

I was the only apprentice on board. The rest of them were on leave and I had it all to myself. The following morning, I was up at 7 o'clock to start work and the bosun of the ship came along and told me what I had to do. General dogsbody. Mundane jobs. Sweeping things up. Mostly shovelling coal down in the 'tween decks and it didn't fit in with my idea of going to sea. Went to the galley for food. Hunger is good source and I ate what was before me.

Eventually the rest of the Apprentices joined the ship. She was undocked. We took stores on board and got ready to put to sea. We steamed out from the docks at Cardiff on a cold, wet, miserable, windy November evening and finally got out in the Barry Roads. We had a cargo of Welsh coal. Welsh coal is the finest ever and was exported all over the world. Beautiful fuel but very dirty. We were black men before we became white again. Fresh water in my early days was very limited. In later years we were able to make our own water. They did that from the main engine exhaust. Heat it up and condense it into steam. It was soft. It was good.

As luck would have it, we ran straight into a south-west gale that was blowing right up the Bristol Channel. It took us days and days to get clear of the Bristol channel. As soon as she got a little way down the channel, she started to buck into it. Ferocious seas. The ships then you know were underpowered. Her maximum speed was around nine knots and in ballast she had no rip on the water. The propeller was out of the water half the time.

We were making a light ship passage and were bound for Key West for orders. Key West was at the tip of the Florida Keys in the U.S. Ships used to usually steam towards there until they got their orders by radio. We were up and down and up and down in an awful south-west gale. It was really bad weather. I was shovelling coal into the coal bunkers as they burned it down below in the boiler rooms. I was sick as a dog. I had brand new oil skins on that were so stiff they were like cardboard. The only button I could fasten on them was the top button. All the rest was blown open and I was wet from the neck down. I need not have been wearing them at all. There was no let up. You were kept at it. I was spewing on the coal and it also went into the bunker. At the end of the day at 5 p.m. you knocked off. I was on day work. I was not on watch then. By which time I was as black as the ace of spades from coal dust. The facilities for getting a bath were limited. We had a bucket of water to get washed in and try to get the coal dust off. Our clothes were wet and there was no way you could get them dry.

We had that kind of procedure for three or four days. Life, believe me, was damn miserable. If I had had my way, I would have just got into my flipping bunk but the senior Apprentices used to come along and say "out." I was so sick and weary and home sick that if I could have got my foot on dry land that would have been the end of my sea career. I began to realise I am on my own for the first time. When we would pass the Hook going to America it took about ten days. The Hook was a dangerous place. How far you can see a Lighthouse varies. Some as far as twenty- five miles. The ordinary ones about fifteen miles.

After three days battling against a southwest gale, we finally got into open water and eventually the weather cleared. Things brightened up as we got west of the Azores and we finally got to Key West and got orders to proceed to Galverston, Texas to load scrap iron and cotton for Japan.

We sailed from Galverston, through the PANAMA CANAL, which was a fantastic experience. It was an eye opener to me as it would be to anybody else on their first transit of it. I was really impressed by all the technology and how the ships went into the locks and were raised up and down and eventually we reached the other side which was Panama City where we dropped our Pilot and then we set off into the Pacific. By that time, I was a watch keeper and I was able to steer the ship. I was on watch which consisted of four on and four off. You did four hours on and you had four hours below where you mainly slept. Then you came on again, so you did quite long hours during the day. You got used to the routine.

The heat was another problem. I remember when we got there the black canal gangs used to come aboard to work the ship through the canal and used to bring massive hanks of bananas with them. They used to barter them well for pretty much nothing and there used to be bananas all over the place. Of course, we made beasts of ourselves and got sick, had tummy troubles and all the rest of it.

Our first port of call after we left the Panama was Los Angeles which we called in to take on our bunkers, that is fuel to fire the boilers, and we were there about six or seven hours. Then we sailed from there and set out across the Pacific towards Japan. We passed through the Hawaiian islands and crossed the South Pacific and finally arrived at our port of call, which was Kobe in Japan where we discharged our cargo.

JAPAN FIRST TIME

First port of call Kobe. January 1935. The Japan of those days was an entirely different proposition to the Japan of the present day. You couldn't compare it. That goes for every country of course. Japan was a very lovely country. Very gifted, hardworking people. Very gentle people. The real Japan as I thought. There were little bars and we all had Japanese girlfriends. They were charming and very good to us. There was very little western influence in those days but the war changed everything. It brought out the latent savagery which was in them. Very cruel. Massacred hundreds, thousands.

One of the first things that impressed me then was everybody was so colourful. The women especially. They all wore beautiful kimonos and the men wore the Japanese traditional dress. In the early thirties Japanese were always dressed in their kimonos and depending on your stature in life the better your clothes reflected your prosperity and your honour.

They did not wear shoes as such. They used to wear what we called clip clops on their feet. A flat piece of board with two upright pieces of board. Leather strap. In their homes they wore decorated slippers, all homemade. On market day the sound of the wooden shoes making a clip clopping noise as they walked in the illuminated market was most impressive. Stalls selling all kinds of things I had never seen before. Very cheap. We had our chow and we did not rob them neither. China, everything electrical.

The number of tea- sets I bought. I loaded up with them. We had them in Thomas Street and I bought three or four Japanese dolls in glass cases. How the hell I ever brought them home I do not know. In those days there used to be seventeen yen to the pound. My draw in Japan, when I got a sub there, was a pound but we made a few bob selling scrap brass that we had collected from the scrap iron cargo. There was a lot of brass in amongst it and we collected it in bags and sold it. I suppose we ended up with about fifty yen, which was a lot of money in those days and boy we had a rare old time in Japan. Although we could not speak Japanese it did not stop us getting along.

I really enjoyed my first visit to Japan. I was really impressed indeed but the war changed all that.

CHINA

China was very interesting but very poor. A lot of hardship. A lot of starvation. The Chinese had no use whatsoever for the Japanese.

We eventually finished our discharging and sailed off, ballast passage again for Vancouver to load grain for the U.K. The passage from Japan to British Columbia is always pretty rough and miserable. You are away up North there, as far North as the Aleutian Islands

VANCOUVER

We got to Vancouver in the end and we had to be ready to load grain. This meant you had to erect a lot of wooden fixtures in the ship to divide the ship longitudinally in half and build boxes in the 'tween decks to control the grain. It was loose grain of course.

I was very impressed by Canada. The size of the country. The marvellous scenery going up the Puget Sound, picking up the Pilot at Victoria and getting up to Vancouver to start to load the grain. In those days it used to take about a week and so we had time to take a look around. We were quite impressed.

The Canadians in those days were very friendly people. We eventually set off from Vancouver on our way back to the U.K. and of course back through the Panama Canal and the Caribbean. Eventually we came back to London and discharged our grain.

At the end of my time on the Queen City I was in London again discharging grain. I was promised leave and could go home and leave the ship and rejoin another ship at the end of my leave. Leave, of course, was at the Company's discretion. They could give you a week or two weeks. It all depended on how it suited them. I was informed in London I had to pack my bag, leave the ship and go across to Rotterdam to join another ship that was short of apprentices due to one or two of them being ill. So I got no leave. I was yanked off the Queen City and I was heartbroken about that.

The ship I was to join in Rotterdam was the Sacramento Valley. A nice name but an awful ship. When I arrived over there, she was loading coal. I had a chip on my shoulder from the word go. When I got on board, I was given the worst bunk in the half deck. The half deck was where the apprentices lived. When I looked at the bunk there was a screen door in it and I said to one of the apprentices, "What is that screen door doing in that bunk there?" "That is the Chief Officer's mosquito door. He always keeps that door there." "Am I supposed to sleep in the bunk with that?" "Oh sure yes. The last fellow did." "Well, I'm not!" I got the damn screen door and I chucked it out on number three hatch on top of the coal and left it. Of course, that did not endear me to the Chief Officer. From that moment onwards he never had a good word for me.

The Skipper was an old fella. He hated the Irish. He had no love for any Roman Catholic. I was never one to push my faith and make a show but he knew I was Catholic and boy I got a dog's life. It lasted all the time I was on that ship. I was damn glad to get off it eventually. After we left Rotterdam we went again across to the Gulf of Mexico and discharged cargo in Houston.

IN THE DOGHOUSE

The apprentices in those days were always at war with the deck crew. The able seamen, the ordinary seamen, the deck boys. There was always battles going on between us.

We went ashore in Houston. We used to go ashore in a body. There were always five of us. An apprentice always got the job as night watchman. He had to be on board and look after the ship during the hours of darkness. Anyway, there were five of us ashore and we met this bunch of seamen from our ship and of course a row started and we all started to fight. There was a great to-do. There was an ordinary seaman who I did not particularly like and I was having a go at him and he was having a go at me. After we eventually got back to the ship, in various states of disrepair, this ordinary seaman went up to the Chief Officer and complained that I had attacked him with no provocation. Well, you know we did not need any provocation. They were all at it. So, I was called up to the Captain to be logged and the usual. This ordinary seaman was up there telling his story to the Captain what I had done to him. "You are a bloody liar," I said. "I did not pick on you. There were about ten people engaged in that fracas." "You're a damn liar." "I am not a liar" he said. With that I hauled up and hit him in front of the Captain. So that finished me. I was really in the doghouse then. Anyway, I survived and eventually I finished my time on the ship.

On one occasion we were up in British Columbia, around Vancouver Island, in a place called Crofton. We were loading a full cargo of logs for Sydney, Australia. You always loaded those things at wooden jetties and the logs were all around the ship. They used to stretch for hundreds and hundreds of yards around you. You just picked the logs straight out of the water and on to the ship.

Well at the time Ginger Kirwan was on board with me. He was from Wexford. We were young fellas serving our time as apprentices. When evening came, we used to stop work. We noticed there were little motorboats that the loggers used to push the logs around on the outskirts of the log booms. We decided that when they knocked off and it got dark, we were going to walk across the logs, get into the boats and have a scooch for ourselves. So, after knock-off time and when things had quietened down, Ginger and I set off walking across the logs. It was ok when we were walking across the logs while they were tightly packed but as we approached the perimeter of the log booms there was quite a lot of extra movement and the logs began to roll. We tried to turn back but it was too late then. We eventually ended up in the water and I can tell you it was freezing cold and we did not stay in it very long. It was wintertime. There was snow all over the place. We climbed out of the water on to the logs and lost no time getting across the logs and back to the ship. The Chief Officer of the ship had spotted us. He was ready to send out a rescue party but he saw us coming back. He tore a strip off us as soon as we got on board but we were shivering – really in a state of shock. Anyway, he was good enough. He brought us in and gave us two big stiff glasses of rum. It was entirely against the rules and regulations to give apprentices drink.

SYDNEY JUMPING SHIP FOR THE LADIES – ALMOST

We set off from Crofton and after a long voyage across the Pacific from north to south we eventually arrived at Sydney and went up to a place – it's up past Sydney Bridge – a place called Snails Bay. We anchored there and started to discharge our logs. It was a very leisurely process. People were not in a desperate hurry in those days.

We had quite some time there. It gave Ginger and me enough time to get acquainted with a couple of young girls ashore. We got very interested in them I can assure you and he and I decided that well look we'll jump ship here and see what we can do. The families of the girls had promised us jobs on the railroad. They were apparently railroad people. Ginger and I were all kind of keen to do this. But as the sailing day approached our resolution and our nerve began to desert us and when that ship sailed from Sydney, Ginger and I were still on it. We often wondered what the girls and their families had to say about us.

IN IT FOR THE MONEY

Still on board that same ship we had another incident. It was cold weather again and at the time we were burning oil in the furnaces. It got so cold the flipping oil more or less solidified in the deep tanks and of course the ruddy ship came to a full stop. Well, it ended up that all of the Apprentices, some of the seamen, the Chief Engineer and some of his junior Engineers had to strip off ruddy well naked, wrap a bit of burlap around our private parts and crawl down into the double bottoms into the oil. We had to crawl through the double bottoms (which you probably are aware of are honeycombed with steel floors and transoms and stuff like that) get in there and literally bail the semi solid oil into the suction bay so the pump could take it. We were doing that for days and days and days.

Us apprentices were paid the magnificent sum of sixpence an hour overtime for that job. When I think of the risks of doing a job like that today I am horrified. We were in there with electric lights on long leads and there must have been a lot of gas around and a certain amount of sparks. Anything could have happened. But not a damn thing did happen except we used to come out and literally had to have a bath in paraffin to get this oil off us. God knows what kind of damage that must have done to our skin. At least it did not do any permanent damage. But it just goes to show you the kind of things that went on years ago.

By the way after that voyage, it was realised that Ginger Kirwan was colour blind and that was the end of his sea going days. He did not go to sea anymore. He was very disappointed about it but if you were colour blind the theory was you could not distinguish the lights of an oncoming vessel, but I do not think it was all that important.

SANTA CLARA VALLEY

I was in London on a ship called the Santa Clara Valley, one of the first motor ships that Reardon Smiths had and she was quite a nice ship too. We had finished a voyage back from the west coast of the U.S.A. We had been to Honolulu and had a very nice cargo of tinned fruit. In fact, us apprentices pretty much lived on the damn stuff. We were sick of it. Of course, it was broached cargo. We had knocked it off. If you were discovered doing that in those days it meant the cancellation of your indentures. But we were not caught. We were too cute to be caught.

BROTHER JIM TUBERCULOSIS IN LOS ANGELES

I was on a ship loading general cargo, mostly tinned fruit and stuff, in the Port of Los Angeles. It was San Pedro. I heard through the Agent that the Devon City was due the following day. I knew my brother Jim was fourth Engineer on that ship and I'd heard that he had been ill. I guessed it could have been the scourge of the Higgins family. That was tuberculosis.

I asked permission (I was an Apprentice of course) from the Skipper if he could get me out to meet the ship. The Devon City was coming into bunker. She would not actually be coming alongside. They used to take bunker in those days from barges at anchor. We arranged for me to go out in the launch with the Pilot.

We boarded the ship and I went up and saw the Captain and told him who I was and that I had come to see my brother. He had the Steward bring me down to Jim's cabin. God when I went in poor old Jim was in his bunk and he was literally like death warmed up. He was like a ruddy skeleton. He was obviously in a bad way and I was very concerned about him. He tried to make light of the matter and all the rest of it. He said he had a heavy cold but I knew better. What the Steward told me was that he hadn't been taking his food and had had a few haemorrhages.

I went up on the bridge and saw the Captain of the ship again and said I'd have to land my brother here and put him in hospital right away. He said, "It's not my intention to land your brother. I was going to take him back to England." I said, "If you do, he'll probably be dead by the time you get there." I had quite an argument with him.

Now you can imagine an Apprentice and a Captain of a ship (there is quite a difference). Trying to talk this fellow into my way of thinking was quite an effort. In the end I said I would really insist even if I had to go ashore to the police and the Port Authority. So, he then agreed. He said they would have a Doctor to him and if the Doctor certified that it would be dangerous to carry him any further he would land the man.

Jim, subsequently, was landed and taken into a hospital in Los Angeles. He was in a bad way. Fortunately, the ship that I was on was there for another couple of weeks, so I was able to visit him pretty well every day. I had a lot of time off from the ship. They let me go any time I wanted to.

I saw the Doctor who was attending to Jim and he said it was tuberculosis in an advanced state but it wasn't a hopeless case. I said, "What do you mean by that?" He said, "It will take a long time. It will take six months but I can nearly guarantee that he'll be a fit man at the end of six months. We will keep him here and build up his strength to give him complete rest for several months. We have a sanatorium in Arizona which is pretty dry country and pretty hot. We will send him there and let nature do the rest." That is precisely what happened.

Eventually Jim was repatriated back home. When he arrived in Wexford he was really a fit man. I wasn't there of course but what mother and Agnes told me about him he was the picture of health when he arrived back. But he was told never to go back to sea again. I believe once you have tuberculosis you always have a weakness in your lungs and damp atmosphere really does affect it.

He didn't listen to that advice and after two years the urge came on him. He went back to sea and the same things happened all over again. He came down with tuberculosis. He didn't die at sea. He came home and lived a few months at home and then the poor fellow died.

UP IN THE WORLD

When you finish your apprenticeship, you were promoted to quarter master, which looks like a very exalted rank but actually just a notch above an able seaman. But what I was interested in was that I was getting paid then. I got ten pounds a month for that. My whole pay for the four years as an apprentice was sixty pounds. So, to be paid ten pounds a month I thought I was pretty wealthy. I did three months over my apprenticeship time before we eventually got back to the U.K. The ship paid off and I came home.

COLLEGE INTERUPTED 1939-1945

I started to sit for my Second Mate's certificate. When I say sit, it meant going to College,

I had digs with a relation of mine from Wexford. I remember old Mrs. Walsh very well. She was very kind to me. Her maiden name was O'Rourke. She wasn't really close to us back in Wexford but she was a relation. She was married to Paddy Walsh. I had digs with them and I was very lucky. They treated me very well. She charged me one pound a week for my digs and that included everything. Washing, laundry, the lot.

Unfortunately, that was around about the outbreak of the second World War. We were in College and I remember the month of August the College used to close down for the summer holidays. That to me was a dead loss because I just had sufficient money to last me so long. I had to do something in that period otherwise I'd have to go back to sea to earn some more money. There was no dole in those days. You were entirely on your own and, of course, I could not expect any financial assistance from home. So, I had to do it all more-or-less by myself.

MANCHESTER ON GIRL'S BIKE, KUFHRA BLOWN UP

There was a Shipping Company run out of Manchester in those days and they used to do twenty- eight-day trips from Manchester to Montreal and Quebec and back. There were some Apprentices in the College with me that belonged to this firm – Manchester Liners – and they said they were going to do this trip across to Montreal and back for the same reason that they were after the money. They asked me if I wanted to go – "You will get a job there all right."

So now I had to get to Manchester. I borrowed a bicycle from my digs. It was a girl's bicycle. I rode all the way to Manchester and saw the Marine Superintendent. He gave me the job and told me to be back the following Monday to join the ship. I cycled back from Manchester to Liverpool. That is a fairly good ride I can tell you. I think it's about thirty miles. I got my gear together and scraped up sufficient cash to get a bus back up on the Monday morning and eventually made the trip across to Montreal on that ship. The Manchester Progress was the name of the ship. She carried twelve passengers.

I remember the first night out after we left Manchester. We cleared the Liverpool bar and went up North. We ran into bad weather north off Ireland and the passengers were all sick. The food that was cooked for their dinner was not required. So, the dogsbodies got the food. Believe me it was a big improvement to what we would have got but from then on we were back to square one, back to the normal ration.

I paid off that ship with about eleven pounds if I remember rightly, which was again quite a bit of money in those days. It gave me at least eight weeks studying time and I resumed studying again. But then the damn war got going and all our lecturers in the College – most of them were R.N.R. fellows – were called up and again the College was closed down.

So, the only thing I could do was go back to sea. I went down and applied to the Shipping Companies and eventually joined a Company called Moss Hutchinson as an A.B. The ship was fitting out to carry case octane from Swansea across to France to a place called Brest and Nantes. The octane was for the Air Force and she was fitting out to carry this cargo so she was there for several weeks.

Whilst I was there, I was told by the Naval Authorities to take a gunnery course. I went down to the H.M.S. Elith, as she was then, in Liverpool and took a crash course in how to fire a flipping gun. The gun I was trained on was a 4.7 and this was the kind of gun that was also installed on the ship I was about to join. The ship was called Kufhra.

KUFHRA – A POTENTIAL BOMB

We sailed from Liverpool down to Swansea and started to load our first cargo of octane. The octane used to be carried in two- gallon tins and there were four tins to a wooden crate. The tins were just paper thin and a lot of them leaked. The octane as it leaked turned into gas and all the holds were absolutely full. She was a potential bomb. I realised what I had joined then.

She had been filled with steam injectors in the hold and the idea was to pump steam into the hold to eject the petrol fumes but it never worked. We set off with this lot across the Channel. The voyage was uneventful. We got to Brest and discharged our cargo. We did several trips like that and there were three or four other ships involved with us. We did not see much enemy action.

It was a phoney war then. I used to practise with the 4.7 gun firing shells out of it. I do not suppose I would ever have hit anything, but it did a lot for my morale and I think the morale of everyone else. I had to train a crew to man this gun from the ordinary fellows. This was the only protection we had.

SHIP IN FRONT OF US BLOWN UP

On the fourth trip across we were at anchor. There was another ship in the berth discharging the same cargo and we were watching her discharge. The next thing there was an almighty bang and a flash and flames all over the place. When this lot cleared there was no ship left. The cargo of octane had exploded.

A lot of men lost their lives there. They managed to drag what was left of the hulk clear of the berth and we were the next ship in. We were discharging the same cargo so you can imagine how we felt about this lot. They took very stringent precautions after that and we discharged ok. There were no casualties. But we were glad to see the last case of petrol go off and get clear of the berth again.

WHAT WAR COULD BE LIKE

It was a very, very, hazardous, a very foolhardy way of conveying that kind of volatile liquid across to the Air Force. It should have been really entangled but of course they didn't have those kinds of things in those days. They have to use whatever they had. There were no real precautions taken.

Soldiers used to come on board to discharge the ship and they would be wearing hob nailed boots. There were steel bands across the ends of the hatches and the cranes all had chains hanging out of them, which used to rattle on the hatch covers. You could see them sparking. We must have been lucky. The good Lord was looking after us. But it was not a very pleasant sight to see a ship that used to be company with us being blown apart. We knew pretty much everyone on that ship. It did bring home what war could be like.

SKIPPER TOOK A SHINE TO ME

I think I did another three or four trips on the Kufthra and then decided to leave. The College had reopened in Liverpool and I decided I would go back and resume my studies. Incidentally, the Skipper of this Kufhra was a Cork man and I suppose because I came from Wexford and all the rest, he took a shine to me.

He said, "As soon as you get your certificate you get in touch with me and I will make sure you get a job with this Company." I did not get in touch. I did not like the trade. They were Mediterranean traders. I wanted to go a little bit further afield than that. He was a hell of a nice fellow. I do not know whether he survived the war or not, but the ship was cut in two by a British destroyer during the evacuation of France and there was quite a loss of life.

SECOND MATE'S CERTIFICATE

I came back to Liverpool and picked up the threads of my study and eventually got my Second Mate's Certificate. That was great and I was very pleased about that.

The war had started to hot up now. There were bombing raids going on and all the rest of it. There were one or two exciting nights even in Liverpool in those days. It did not affect me too much. I seemed to be able to get on with my studies. I did not have too many problems with my exam and eventually got it.

I decided to go home for a holiday. I think Patty was on her last legs, poor girl. She was dying of tuberculosis, as Teddy before her. But before I did go home poor Patty died. I did get back for the funeral. It was a very sad time. Mother did not want me to go to sea again while the war was on. I was between the devil and the deep blue sea literally because I did not want to stay in Wexford. I wanted to go back to sea. Strangely enough I rather enjoyed the war time excitement. I just could not get away. I had not the heart to say, "Well I am going back," so I just hung around for a few weeks.

WEXFORD COASTERS

In those days Staffords had a couple of coasters running out of town. Harry Wilson had two ships called the Goldfinder and the Beag Erin. One day he actually came up the house and asked, "Look, would you be interested in taking the Mate's job on the Goldfinder as the present Mate is ill?" I jumped at the chance at getting to sea again, even if it was only around the coast. Those ships by the way – Wilson ships – flew the British flag. I think they were partially owned by someone in the Bristol Channel but they were under the British flag. So, I went.

We eventually sailed. I was Mate of this thing. The whole complement of the ship was about seven. The Skipper of the ship was a hell of a nice fella. One of the nicest fellas I have ever sailed with and a hell of a good seaman but he like his booze. We set off. In those days we used to take loads of spuds and stuff over to the Bristol Channel. Even up to Liverpool as cargo and we would load coal in England and take it back, usually to Wexford and discharge there.

Sometimes we used to have to go into Rosslare Harbour, into the Pier, to lighten up to get over the bar into Wexford. She was not all that big I can assure you. I think there were times then there was only seven or eight feet of water on the bar.

Mother was quite happy with me being on that ship as it did not go very far and was not in any danger. We were up and down the Irish Sea. Well away from the submarines and things like that.

Anyway, I do not think a sub would have wasted a torpedo on us.

I quite enjoyed the time on that ship but it was absolutely, deadly boring. Say you were going into Newport in the Bristol Channel for a load of coal. You would go there on the top of the tide and you would sail on the following tide. You were in port for about twelve hours loading. You used to go underneath the coal tips and they would empty forty-ton wagons into the ship. She only had a capacity of about 400 tons of cargo and she was loaded in no time. Then you had to pull off the berth and wait for the lock gates to open at tide time and you were out and down the Bristol Channel again on your way back to Wexford.

MATE TOO MUCH TO DRINK

When you got back to Wexford the stevedores were waiting on the quayside. You had to have your hatches open and everything ready for them before you got alongside. As you were tying the ship up alongside, they were throwing their shovels aboard. They used to be paid piece money and so it did not take them long to discharge that ship. You had about twenty- four hours in Wexford and then you were back out again. This was how life went on.

Sometimes you had bad weather and bad weather in those ships was pretty grim. You would have no comfort whatsoever. You supplied your own food and it was the youngest member of the crew who was expected to cook it. You can bet your boots our table requirements were pretty basic. As I say, in bad weather it used to be pretty grim.

The Skipper, as soon as he got into port he would be up to the nearest pub and he used to get well oiled. I would load the ship and then we would have to go in search of him. We brought him back much worse for the drink and put him in his bunk.

I WOULD SAY YES

The Agent used to give me the papers and he would say, "You're going to so and so" and I would sail the ship. The Skipper would be in his bunk blotto! We came from the Bristol Channel back to Wexford and I would see him just appear again on the bridge about five minutes before we had to get to the Wexford bar and he would say, "Mark are we bound for Wexford this time?" and I would say, "Yes."

Another case, we were leaving Dublin and he was carried on board in a similar state. We were bound for Cork this time. We sailed and were going down the coast around the Tuskar and he made his appearance on the bridge and said, "Where are we bound this time Mark?" You know he did not give a damn. He used to take everything in his stride like that.

KEEN IN THOSE DAYS

I was very keen in them days. I was a brand-new second Mate. I had a sextant on the ship and sometimes I did not bother about coasting as the coasting crowd do. They do not lose sight of the land or the landmarks. If we left Wexford and we were bound for Liverpool I would not go up as far as Dublin and then cross to say the South Stack and from there on into Liverpool Bay. I would make a direct course from Wexford straight up to the South Stack.

I would use my sextant. It was hardly worthwhile using but I used to use it. Old Phil used to be pretty impressed by this and it used to save us a few hours too on the journey.

Wilson wanted me to stay in that Company with them and he promised me a Master's job on one of the coasters within months if I stayed. I was supposed to get my Pilot's licence for Liverpool and my Pilot's licence for the Bristol Channel and I was supposed to get my Pilot's licence for up around Glasgow.

The coasters used to trade regularly to those ports and were allowed to do their own piloting. Wilson said, "You have the capacity to do that and you're going to save me some money and you will make a few bob on it too."

I took it all into consideration but I wanted to get deep water again, so I left the Goldfinder and told Mother. By now she had got more or less resigned to it and didn't put up too much of a fight. I eventually took off again.

ENSIGNE MARIE ST. GERMAIN. TOUGH TIME

The next ship I joined was a French coaster on the Tyne. She was a big one mind, about five thousand tonnes. All she had ever carried in her life was coal. When the British Army was run out of Dunkirk the free French brought her over to the U.K. She came under the British flag. British crewed. Our firm Reardon Smith took her over.

My first job on her was Third Mate. When I found out what we were going to be doing I was not very pleased at all. We were going to load coal at the Tyne, take it down to London, come back from

London to the Tyne and upwards and down all the while just carrying coal to the power stations in the London docks. We were on that for twelve months. I stayed for twelve months on that ship. That was one of the toughest twelve months I had pretty well during the war.

GERMANS BOMBING US

On the first occasion we sailed out of the Tyne with a load of coal for London there were two or three ships with us. We anchored outside, about a mile off Tyne Piers, waiting for the main convoy to come down from the North. By this time, the Navy had put naval personnel on the ships to help out with the defence of the Merchant ships. Our armament on that ship consisted of two beat up old Hotchkiss guns and a portable bren gun. The bren gun was my responsibility. We had a twelve pounder on the poop that was never used.

We were at anchor off the Tyne Piers. There were three ships with us. I was in the bridge and the two naval gunners were up on the bridge with me at the same time. Next thing we heard the roar of aircraft engines. You automatically manned your guns until you identified the sound. It was day light, just getting on for sunset and straight out of the sun came two German bombers. Dorniers they were. They were flying about fifty feet over the water and came straight out of the sun. They were coming hell bent towards us. We got firing the two Hotchkiss and the bren gun at them. You fired a hell of a lot of tracers in those days and it used to make quite a show. One of the bombers was more or less headed towards us and the other fellow was headed towards another ship in the convoy.

As the fellow that was attacking us came in, I think he lost his nerve a bit because he seemed to bank away from us and as he banked away, he let go his bombs. It was a stick of five and they did not straddle us but fell up and down alongside the ship, I would say about fifty yards off. There was hell fire and bloody explosions all over the place. We were covered in bloody seawater - the spray that came up from the explosions. And then he was gone. We did not hit him. I do not think we put a shot into him. It was too quick but I think we startled him.

DIRECT HIT

The other bomber scored a direct hit. He put his five bombs right up and down one of the other ships and really made a mess of her. As the smoke settled and we got our breath back we had a look at this other ship and she was on fire, fore and aft. We launched our lifeboat and rowed across to her. We did not have power boats in those days. We had to pull this lifeboat across.

We got on board the ship and she was burning pretty fiercely. There were a lot of people killed on her and a hell of a lot of people injured. There was blood and gore all over the place. We did what we could for them but the ship was sinking underneath our feet. A couple of armed trawlers came rushing out of the Tyne and came alongside. We had injured on the lifeboat, which we had taken off. The trawlers took off the remaining people. As we got clear of that ship (we were just standing off watching what was going on) she went down. Sank there and then. We landed our injured onto one of the armed trawlers and they took them right back into port. We went back to the ship.

DEAD FISH FOR SUPPER

One of the things that impressed me, that stood out in my mind as we were going back, was the number, the mass of dead fish that was floating on top of the water. All kinds of fish. I remember some of the fellows picking them up and throwing them into the bottom of the boat. I think we had them for our supper a couple of days later.

E BOATS ATTACK

That was a sample of what life was going to be like for the next twelve months. It was a really a rough time on that east coast I do not mind telling you. On the way down to London we used to be attacked by E boats. They used torpedoes on us and machine guns. If it was not bloody E boats it was bombers flying over and letting go at us.

One of the other things we had to contend with was mines. There were mines all over the place. We used to have to stick to swept channels and the channels were buoyed so you would not stray out of them. If you strayed out of the channels you were in minefields, both British and German. It was essential that you stayed in the swept channels. The channels used to be swept as you were actually proceeding down. In the channels you would have the minesweepers working up ahead of you. If you strayed out at all you were in real trouble.

One of the tricks that the E boats used to get up to was, in the hours of darkness, they would come along and change the characteristics or even shift the buoys. They used to have cutting gear on board and they used to move the buoys out of position so as to put you into a minefield or something. They were up to all kinds of bloody tricks. It used to be hair raising I can assure you. They used to combine an E boat attack with a bombing attack. That usually happened at dusk or at dawn. You got the E boats coming in from the north sea. The bombers over your head. You did not know what to shoot at. The bombers had a trick of flying down between the columns of the convoy.

BOMBING DOWN MIDDLE OF CONVOY

There were two lines of ships in the coastal convoy so there was just the one column in the middle. I have seen German bombers fly down at ship level. Right down the middle between the ships. Of course, you could not really fire at the buggers because if you did you were firing at your friends on the other side. They used to use their machine guns at us as they swept down. They used to do that after they had dropped their bombs. They used to make strafing runs down the middle.

They must have been bloody brave men because in the end the instructions went out that you were to fire on them regardless of the people on the other side.

We must have shot up a lot of our ships trying to knock the bombers down. I have seen quite a few of the bombers go down but there were so many ships firing on them you could not really tell who really did knock them out. The E boats could take a lot of light machine gun fire but it was nearly impossible to hit them with a twelve pounder so nobody tried too hard. You used to try to keep them at a distance with whatever light armament you had but they caused a hell of a lot of damage, I don‘t mind telling you.

THE PATTERN OF LIFE, BOMBS ALL OVER THE PLACE

That was the pattern of life. That is what it was like up and down the east coast. We had that for twelve months. Then, when we got to London to our discharging berth, which was really right in the heart of London, you used to get the London blitzes. There used to be bombs all over the place, falling all around you. The ship I was on must have had a ruddy charmed life. She was never hit. Hit by machine gun fire and light stuff but nothing really serious. The ship had a beautiful name. She was called the Enseigne Marie St. Germain. Now a ship with a name like that you would imagine she was a beautiful, yacht-looking creature. She was anything but. She was a snub nosed and stub stern old collier but she was a lucky ship. When I left her she was intact. She was subsequently mined. She had a near miss with a mine on the same run, someway of the Humber but they beached her and got her off and she was repaired and finished the war.

FRENCH DO NOT DRINK WATER

The story about that ship was we took her over pretty much straight from the French. The last crew that was on her before we took her over were a French crew. The good thing about it was they left casks and casks of white and red rough wine. You know the French do not drink any water. We had an unlimited supply of wine and that did more for our morale than anything else.

YAN THE MOST AMAZING FRENCH DOG WHO CAME TO ENGLAND

The French crew also left us their French dog. He was called Yan. The Second Mate and I had full charge of him. Yan could only bark in French. We had to teach him English so he could bark in English. He eventually took to us. He was particularly attached to me and the Second Mate and we looked after him. If the Second Mate was on watch he would be up there with him and myself also if I was on watch. He was a lovely, lovely animal. He was never fazed by the bombing on the ship, as long as we were there along with him.

A bomb one night meant Arkwright, the Second Mate, was trapped when a wardrobe fell off the wall with the blast and the dog was with him. The wardrobe was dragged off him. The dog did not panic. He was not worried about the bombs going off all around him as long as we were there with him. Most dogs are terrified of noise. I could never get over that dog. In the course of the voyage, he developed a growth on his shoulder so when we got back to South Shields we took the dog to the vet and the vet said it looks to me as though he has a cancerous growth and if it is removed he will have a good chance of survival. We left him with the vet asking him to do the best he could for him.

We sailed off again and when we got back he had had his operation. When we went to collect him, he was wrapped up in a bandage and he was beautiful and clean, lovely. When he saw the two of us he licked us all over. We were told he was fine but to keep on the bandage. We took him back to the ship. As soon as he got back he rolled all over the ship and was black as the ace of spades in ten minutes. Rolling in the coal dust he just loved. He was only happy on the ship. If we took him for a walk when we docked he wasn't happy. The final story is that Arkwright left that ship after I did and he took the dog with him to his home. He lived somewhere around Middlesbrough, I think, and that dog lived for quite a few years after that. The same Second Officer, Arkwright, was in later years Captain on the cross-channel ferry boat between Fishguard and Rosslare. I met him as we went backwards and forwards. We always talked of the dog and our time on the St. Germaine.

SHIP BLOWN APART

On one occasion in convoy on the way down to London I was on the bridge with the Skipper. There was a ship ahead of us - in the same convoy of course. We were about seventy-five yards from her stern. You had to keep close. You could not straggle. You had to keep as tight as possible so as the escorts could give you maximum protection. We used to have five or six destroyers escorting us down and the orders were always to keep bunched up close as possible, which we did. But this ship, it was night-time and we were following this fellow. They used to carry a small, very dim stern light. It was usually a blue light and it was very dim. We could see it on the following ship and we were keeping our eye on this ship.

The next minute there was an almighty bloody explosion and the whole sky lit up and I thought we had hit a mine but the ship ahead had hit a mine and it really made a mess or her. She was damn near blown apart. We sailed right through a lot of the wreckage of that ship because we had no time to do anything to avoid her. We were scraping against all kinds of bits and pieces. I did not actually hear anyone in the water or anything because the noise had more or less deafened us but we must have sailed through people that night and I don't suppose those poor fellows were ever picked up. They were left to die there and die a lonely death. In normal times you would stop and pick them up. They fought for their country and died.

We learned afterwards that most of the crew on that ship had been killed. That kind of experience was not something that rarely happened. You used to get it in every convoy but not as close as it was that time. You would see an explosion in the convoy and a mass of flames and you knew it was a ship had hit a mine. They used to have drifting mines. Even though the drifting mines were not as dangerous to a ship as a moored mine, they still could be bad.

As I say life on that coast could be hectic. From time to time, you left the Tyne until you reached London. It used to take us two and a half days to do the journey. You never got out of your clothes. You never took your Mae West off. When you lay down to sleep you slept in your clothes. By the time you got to your destination you were beginning to smell pretty high to say the least but that was the least of our worries. We were glad to get to the bloody place and get a little respite. You used to catch the air raids in port.

THE GOOD TIMES - SOUTH SHIELDS, THE TYNE

We used to have some good nights ashore in the different ports. People, especially around South

Shields and the Tyne, were very friendly and they gave us a good time. We were ashore pretty much every night and we used to get tanked up. There were dances and we were out with the girls. It was a great life. Pretty colourful. I think people were trying to get away from the anxieties of war and all the rest of it. When they went out to enjoy themselves, believe me, they really did.

I had some wild nights in South Shields and to a certain extent in London too. The Grosvenor Hotel in London was patronised a lot by the Navy. Lots of the merchant service used to get in there too. There used to be great goings on there. Impromptu sing songs and plenty to drink. Everybody was quite happy.

Many a night I was normally ashore with a sail mate. The two of us came out and we did not have a hope in hell of getting back to the ship. All transport like the tubes and the trains had packed in for the night. They might have packed in anyway if there was an air raid on but we used to get back. I came down from London on a goods train and, you know, the drivers and guards were only too damn happy to pick you up and give you a lift back. There was a great spirit then. People you know they would do a lot for you.

Rules and regulations did not count for much. If somebody thought they could help you out by letting you ride a goods train back to your destination, well things like that used to happen. I look back with a lot of pleasure on those days.

AND THE BAD

There were some awful scenes too. I remember one night we were in South Shields, alongside the coal stage and partially loaded. There was a hell of an air raid over the Tyne area. South Shields got it very badly. There was over four hundred people killed in one shelter that night. It was kind of an underground shelter in the main square of the town (the old marketplace of the town) and there was a graveyard hit at the same time. I remember we were on the ship. I do not know what we were doing. I suppose we were terrified but the A.R.P. Warden came down looking for assistance to give them a hand to try and get those people out of the underground shelter that had been hit. We went in there and the scenes were horrific. We had to pass by this graveyard on the way there and believe me, not a word of a lie, there was all kinds of bits of bones and skulls all over the place. The bomb that hit that graveyard had certainly opened up that graveyard and spread the remains of people that have been in that place for hundreds of years all over the place. But the actual underground shelter that had been hit was very horrific. It had gone on fire and we were there trying to do what the hell we could. It is just something I would sooner not dwell on too much. There were some ruddy awful scenes that night.

After I left Enseigne St. Germain of famous memory I came back to Wexford for a few weeks holiday. The parents were not too keen on me going back again but I did not hang around and I went back.

BARRGROVE – CARGO YOU NAME IT WE CARRIED IT

My next ship was called Barrgrove. Not one of Reardon Smith's ships. She was a British ship but she was managed by Reardon Smith. I was appointed Second Mate on this ship and we took off.

We were loading coal. We had a part cargo of coal and on top of that the coal was flattened off in the hold and levelled off. We had tanks, armoured transports, guns and ammunition. You name it we had it. This was destined for Alexandria in Egypt. At that time, the Mediterranean - the western Mediterranean - was a no-go area for British ships so there was no way we were going to go through Gibraltar and proceed towards Alexandria in the normal way. What we had to do was go around the Cape of Good Hope, up the east coast of Africa, through the Red Sea and eventually Alexandria.

THE LONG WAY ROUND

We sailed out of Newport and picked up the convoy in the Bristol Channel. We proceeded south to the latitude of Gibraltar. Then we were told we were on our own. Any ship proceeding south of that would proceed independently, which is what we did. The submarine war for the Germans had not got down there. There was not much activity in the South Atlantic in those days.

We proceeded and called into Cape Town to take on bunkers and stores. We set off again to round the Cape and up the east coast and eventually into the Red Sea and into Port Suez and the Suez Canal in a matter of a few days. So, it was advisable for the heavy ships of the British Navy to get the hell out of it. It did not do any good for our morale to see them coming out of the Mediterranean and us going into it I can assure you. But we carried on and arrived at Alexandria. Eventually got alongside and started to discharge our cargo. The Battle of Alamein was imminent. In fact, it had started when we got to Alex. I think they must have been waiting for us to start.

ALAMEIN

We started to discharge cargo. The tanks and the ammunition. All this good stuff had been put out. I think Alamein is about forty miles - give or take a few miles - from Alex. You could hear the artillery barrage. It was really one of the heaviest barrages of the war up to then. Montgomery kept at this for days and days until he literally punched a hole through the German defence and it was then he started to break out from Alamein. Well, you know the history of it. They ran the Germans right back along the North African coast.

The Germans really did not put up a very big resistance after that. It was all a rear-guard action because the losses that they sustained at Alamein were terrific. They lost most of their armoured stuff and most of their artillery. Their supply lines were severely hampered by the Royal Air Force. They were in a bad way. They only had one thing to do and that was retreat. They keep on retreating and abandoned most of their equipment until they were finally driven out of all of North Africa. They were sandwiched between the Americans and the Americans had landed at Oran and Algiers and were advancing eastwards to meet the British 8th Army marching westwards. The Germans were in between. They did not have much of a hope and were really knocked out.

The Battle of Alamein was the end of it. We were there while that battle was on and you would swear it was just a mile up the road. We were well aware of it because you could see streams of ambulances coming back full of wounded and transports moving backwards and forwards. The Germans were throwing everything they could at us, using their Air Force to try and break down the lines of communications. The docks at Alexandria were really pasted but we were there and had no near misses. We were quite fortunate in that respect. In fact, we had a grandstand view of all the excitement going on.

We finished discharging our cargo. The coal was for the Egyptians and sailed again. We sailed up to Port Said, through the Suez Canal and back out into the Gulf of Suez into the Red Sea.

A very unfortunate thing happened at Port Jufik while we were at Alexandria. A hospital ship that was manned mostly by Royal Naval Wrens, the nursing part of it, had received a direct hit from bombers. There was very heavy loss of life on the ship and it sank. Very unfortunate. As we sailed by you could still see the debris and the remains and bits and pieces floating.

LOURENCO MARQUES

We went down the Red Sea and out into the Indian Ocean and went south again. We had to put into Lourenco Marques for repairs. We had sprung a leak in number one hold. They put about a half dozen new plates in around number one hold. We were there three weeks. She was an old ship, this Barrgrove. She was a WW1 ship, built prior to WW1 and she was really an old rust box but she was a lucky ship.

LIVE AND LET LIVE - DRINKING WITH THE GERMANS

The funny part of our stay in Lourenco Marques was that there were about six or seven German Merchant ships that had been caught in Lourenco Marques when the war broke out and had been interned. The ships were there and the German crews were still on them. Of course we used to go ashore of a night in the local boozers and Christ you would be drinking bloody beer with Germans at the next table. Nobody seemed to pay too much attention to them, and they did not pay too much attention to us. So, it was a case of live and let live.

JAPANESE NAVY BECAME VERY ACTIVE

While we were in Lourenco Marques the Japanese navy became very active in the southern Indian Ocean, especially around Durban and Lourenco Marques. One of our diversions of an evening was to actually watch survivors from Merchant ships being landed. Ships that had been torpedoed by the Japanese submarines. It was very active for the time we were there. So it was with some trepidation that we eventually sailed from Lourenco Marques and proceeded out very apprehensive about all those Japanese submarines out there. Again, we did not see any sign of them and safely got around Cape of Good Hope.

DURBAN CHRISTMAS KINDNESS

Once again, we called into Durban for bunkers. It was just prior to Christmas. I think it was Christmas 1942. The people there, the South Africans, were very kind to us. They absolutely filled the ship with Christmas presents. They gave us everything. We had all kinds of stuff leaving there. We had only called for bunkers so were only there for about twelve hours but during that twelve hours they had us ashore and they put on parties for us and all the rest of it. They were very good to us.

CONVOY FROM HALIFAX NOVA SCOTIA

We eventually set off and proceeded again independently. We were west bound again across to South America. We eventually arrived at Brazil and loaded a cargo of iron ore at one of the ports. This iron ore was destined for the U.K. Now to get to the U.K., we had to sail northwards up the South American coastline, through the Caribbean and up the east coast of the U.S.A., until we finally arrived at Halifax, Nova Scotia. We anchored there and waited for the convoy to form up, which it subsequently did, and we set sail.

Incidentally, the Commander of the actual convoy would be in a Merchant ship and he was referred to as the Commodore. He was an ex naval type. They used to be retired Admirals or retired naval Captains. They used to take charge of the actual convoy from the point of view of signals with the naval escort. The Barrgrove was given the honourable job of Vice Commodore. We had some signallers on board and a Lieutenant - retired Lieutenant I should say - out of the navy. The reason why we had the Vice Commodore was in case the Commodore got pipped. We would then take his place. We set sail about February which was about the worst time to make a western ocean passage. To avoid the submarine packs - the submarines were operating in packs then - we had to proceed up as far north as Greenland and we arrived having hellfire weather there. Gales and you name it we had it, snow, blizzards, the bloody lot.

YOU'VE HAD IT, MARK, SHIP LABOURING

We were about fifty miles south of Cape Farewell in convoy, blowing a heavy gale, blizzards, snow all over the place. The ship was labouring away, with iron ore bloody cargo. I tell you, well, life was not at all pleasant. During the middle of the night our steering gear carried away. That, of course, put us completely out of command we just squared right across the sea and lay wallowing in the swell. She was taking bloody seas all over her. I thought, "You've had it Mark," you know. Being one of the leading ships we really did expect to be run down by ships passing us.

There were several dark shapes loomed out of the blizzard but by God's grace they missed us. Eventually we were left on our own just wallowing away. We were in a bad way. There was nobody to give you any assistance. The rest of them had just gone. There was no communication by radio. You could not send out a message over the air in case you gave away the position of the convoy so you had to remain dumb.

I was Second Mate and the Mate was an elderly man and he was not very active. He was a good sea man and all the rest of it but he was an old man and the job of trying to get the steering gear rigged up - Gerry rigged - was my prerogative.

TOO TERRIFIED TO FEEL ANYTHING

The temperature was well below zero. There was ice all over the place and of course with seas coming on board we on the open deck we were wet from top to bottom. You know I never recollect feeling cold that night. I think I was too bloody terrified to feel anything (chuckle). We tackled this job of getting the rudder under control. As I said, she was an old ship and the old ships used to have massive, big steering wheels right on the poop, double steering wheels. Massive things. By a system of pinions and screws and things you could connect the wheel directly to the rudder but you had to get the quadrant in the right position to do that. If you get the quadrant in the right position, it was a work of art because the rudder was just banging backwards and forwards as the seas hit it. We managed to control the rudder a bit with heavy tackles. We had to try and get it into the midships position so as we could drop the connecting pins into the worn gear to connect the wheels. Well during the process of doing that, say it took us about a few hours, one of the able seamen was hit in the leg by the quadrant. It broke his leg just like you would break a bit of stick. We had to get him out of the way and get him stretchered away and then carry on with the job.

ON COURSE AGAIN

We eventually got the pins in and engaged the steering wheels. It took four men to man those massive wheels. There was just hand steering now, with a little bit of relief from the gearing in the hand gear. We eventually got the engines going and brought her around back up on the course again. It was quite a struggle getting the old girl to come out of the trough but she eventually wallowed out of it and we resumed our course. It was breaking light by now, not that that was making much difference because you could not see much anyway. There was scud and foam and blizzards all over the place.

TAIL OF THE BANK

We set a course and some days later we arrived on all our own at the Tail of the Bank off Grenough and we put the anchor down. Boy I was relieved and so was everybody else on that ship on hearing that anchor dropping out of the hawsepipe. She was there for a couple of weeks. They pretty well had to renew the steering gear.

We were quite proud of ourselves. We had to man that ship - that jury rig - or seven days, I think it was, all by men strength alone. It took four men on that wheel all the while to steer it and that was how she came into the Tail of the Bank right up to the anchorage. We got quite good at it by the time we reached the Tail of the Bank.

On November 12th we eventually took the Barrgrove around the north of Scotland and down the east coast and left her in London. We had the usual attention from the E boats and the bombers on the east coast but we got around ok. The old crew left the ship in London and I came home to Wexford on leave. I did not stay too long in Wexford. I was there a couple of days.

MATE'S CERTIFICATE - BURNING THE MIDNIGHT OIL

I came back to Liverpool to study for my Mate's certificate. Study in war time was a haphazard business. Getting to and from the College was at times a problem but we managed. I had to work pretty hard because I had a time limit on me. I had three months in which to get my certificate, otherwise I would have had to go back to sea again. I remember when I was sitting for my exam. The exam used to take a week. The exams were held in the old Custom House in Liverpool, which was afterwards levelled by bombing but not, fortunately, while we were there.

During the time we were there we had several raids. We used to have to leave the papers where they were in the exam room and go down to the cellars underneath the Custom House and wait until the raid was over. It did not affect me a lot. You knew your concentration was impaired, I suppose, but they allowed you extra time to make up for that.

I used to work weekdays at the college, came home, had my dinner and then I was burning the midnight oil. I busily worked every night up to midnight studying. I used to keep that up all during the week. At the weekends I relaxed a bit. I went to the football match on a Saturday with Calum Powell and we had a few drinks. I still managed to do at least four hours of study on a Saturday and I spent quite some time studying on Sunday. I got my certificate without too many problems and I let the owners, Reardon Smith, know that I was ready for sea again.

FAMILY

Sunday night I used to go and see my lady friend, Babe, across the road and have supper with her. Her mother was a wonderful cook. Believe me, the food was par excellence. I think that was one of the reasons why I married this one (chuckle). She had lovely parents. Her mother was a very nice person and her father, Harry Gray, was one of the best. I remember them with fond memories I can assure you. They were very nice to me and I had a nice time there. Also living in the home was Babe's mother's sister, Stasia, and Rosalie who they fostered. They continued to live with us when Babe's parents died.

AIR RAIDS

During that time Liverpool was having air raids. They were very severe. The docks were pretty well flattened. The ammunition train blew up and there was havoc all over the place.

CHARLIE - TAXI HOME FROM PIER HEAD WHEN HIS SHIP SANK

Another tragic event where nearly half the crew lost their lives in a mine disaster, trapped in their accommodation on the ship and unable to get out before the sea came in. The explosion sank the ship. Charlie said the ship buckled and was on its way down. He was under water the last several feet before he got to the door and out onto the deck. He just fell over the side. The ship had gone from underneath him. He told me he thought he had had it and he did not expect to get out in time. He said he was just about finished but, fortunately, he did get out. As he got over the side, he managed to grab one of the life rafts, which were self-releasing, and just floated off as the ship went down.

He got on to the raft and was eventually picked up by a small tug that towed the raft to the landing stage. You know where the landing stage is, where the ferry boats go backwards and forwards from Liverpool to Birkenhead. They took Charlie and a few other fellows that were on the raft into the landing stage. Arrangements were made to take them to hospital but Charlie did not want to go to hospital. He said, "I want to go home," and he walked up the ramp. There used to be a taxi rank up on the Pier Head. He got into the taxi and told the driver to take him home. He lived only a few miles from the Pier Head.

Classic remark of the taxi driver looking at him as the water was still running out of Charlie's clothes - "You will not be needing that life jacket in the cab as no German submarines have yet surfaced in the middle of Lord Street, chuckle, or other districts of Liverpool."

Strange isn't it? I thought this was a most unusual thing for a fellow whose ship was blown up and sunk and (chuckle) to actually end the adventure by going home by taxi.

Charlie's wife was Secretary in one of the Dock Offices and heard the explosion that sank her husband's ship.

On occasions you would get air raids night after night. Very few people really had a full night's sleep. You were up and in the shelters. Babe and I managed to do our courting with not too much trouble. In fact, we quite enjoyed it. Her father had an Anderson shelter in the back garden and it was very comfortably fitted out. During the air raids we all retired out there. Several of the neighbours too. We all packed in. It was very cosy.

Jack Walsh was the owner of the house where I stayed. He was an Air Raid Warden. I used to go around with him and so did Babe at times. He had a command post in his home. He had a telephone there. He was an important man. We used to all use his telephone for free. It was very interesting. It was also very tragic on occasions when you heard of people you knew being killed.

THE BOMBS COMING DOWN

I remember one night when I was out with Jack. We were in the middle of September Road and there was an air raid on. We heard all these bombs coming down. When you hear bombs coming down you would swear they were going to drop right on top of your head. In this particular case, the bombs dropped on Dunstan Road, which is the bottom of September Road. It just flattened that place down there. We felt the blast where we were in September Road and we were lying flat on the ground. We went down there and Jack got on the 'phone and organised rescue parties. We eventually got down to the scene of the incident and did what we could.

I remember going into one house and finding an old lady still in bed. There was not a scratch on her but she was covered in debris, furniture, all kinds of things were lying across the bed but she had not suffered at all. She did not even appear to be in shock. She probably would have had shock later on. She had a marvellous escape. Those were some of the little incidences that used to occur, which there was no explanation for.

ANGLO AFRICAN

They subsequently appointed me to a ship called the Anglo African. She again was not a real Reardon Smith ship but a ship taken over from another British firm and managed by Reardon Smith for the duration of the war.

I joined her in Cardiff. I was Second Mate now. She was loading stores, ammunition, mines and bombs, all kinds of horrible things, again for the Middle East. This time we took the cargo out through the Straits of Gibraltar. By this time, the allies had regained their superiority in the Mediterranean. The Germans were no longer in North Africa and the Mediterranean. The African coast, east and west, was more or less possible.

CONVOY TO ALEXANDRIA

It was a big convoy, fifty odd ships bound for Alexandria. We were subject to raids as we proceeded eastward into the Mediterranean. Off the North African coast, about one hundred miles west of Algiers, we were again attacked by German bombers. There were even some Italian bombers in this lot. I remember it was a beautiful night, a real moonlight night. It was a night you could well do without in war time because you were sitting ducks. Standing out like sore thumbs.

The Germans then were trying out a new weapon. It was what they called a radio - controlled bomb. They were able to more or less direct the bomb to a target, not just dropping haphazardly on the convoy but aim for a particular ship. They were reasonably successful because in that convoy several tankers and several ships carrying ammunition were hit.

NO SURVIVORS

We were carrying ammunition but they seemed to know which ships to go for. The ship in the column abeam of us, on the inside of us, was an ammunition carrier and she was hit. I have never seen a sight like that before. Talk about pyrotechnics. The whole sky literally lit up. The bloody blast from it. We were abeam of the ship and I suppose about three hundred yards from her. The sea was set up by that explosion. It just hit us. We rolled right over. We must have gone to twenty degrees and back again. But it was not to be. There were no survivors from that ship. In fact, they did not find any part of the ship, let alone survivors.

TORPEDO JUST MISSED US

To add to our worries, this attack on the convoy, as we learned later, was also a combined attack. There were submarines operating too and during the initial mayhem caused by the bombers the subs started to do their bit. I was Gunnery Officer and I was down on the poop. I was manning a twelve-pounder quick firing gun.

We were just shooting straight up into the air. It was what they called barrage fire. You used to pull up fused shells and they exploded at about a thousand feet above the ship. The whole convoy was doing that. The idea, as you probably realised, was to keep the planes above the thousand-foot level so that their accuracy would be somewhat improved and this is what we were doing. Well, we were down all firing this damn gun. As I said it was a clear beautiful night.

The sea in the Mediterranean at certain times of the year was very phosphorescent. The next thing I saw and several other people that were on the gun platform with me saw, was the outline of two torpedoes heading straight for the ship. "Oh, bloody hell. By jeez we cannot miss this one," I said. You could see them as clear as a bell. They were under the water just closing in to us rapidly. The only thing that I could say was, "Down!" and we all lay down. Nothing happened! It would have been within seconds after I said "Down" that we got up gingerly and looked on the other side. You could see the wakes of the torpedoes proceeding across the convoy and they found a target. We do not know what ship it was but in the general line of their direction there was a hell of an explosion. Some poor bastard got it.

WITHOUT ANY FURTHER INCIDENTS

We put into Algiers. We were not bound for Algiers, but the convoy was so disorganised, the losses so heavy, that they had to put into Algiers to reorganise. We were several days in Algiers. We saw quite a few of the survivors, people that had been picked out of the water and picked out of lifeboats and brought into Algiers. Some of them were in a bad way. We were in Algiers a couple of days and then we resumed the convoy to Alexandria where the majority of our cargo was destined for. We subsequently discharged our cargo without any incidents.

HOTEL CECIL ALEXANDRIA

We used to go ashore of a night at Alexandria. There was a Hotel there called Hotel Cecil. It was a favourite watering hole of the armed forces while we were there during the Middle East campaign. I believe the Hotel Cecil is still there. There was a documentary on the television a while ago and I actually saw the Hotel Cecil mentioned. Rather nostalgic. Brought back a few memories. Belly dancing and all kinds of stuff (chuckle). Enough said.

THOUSANDS OF MULES. VERY, VERY SENSIBLE ANIMALS

Our next cargo it was decided we were going to fit out in Port Said to carry mules to support the Eighth Army in Italy. They had originally been part of the British Indian Army. They had set up a big depot of the Indian Army at Beirut. There were thousands upon thousands of mules there. We had the job, with several other ships, to transport those mules to Italy.

We were fitted out to carry a thousand mules at a time, together with their handlers, their fodder and with the motorised transport belongings to the actual division. We made five or six trips altogether. We fitted out and went up to Beirut and it was all set for us to take the mules on board but I am afraid the mules had other ideas.

JOHN WAYNE NEVER SAW THE LIKES OF IT

It was the most amusing time there. They brought those mules down in bunches of twenty - all tethered together. You used to lead them down and try to get them into the nets. The mules wouldn't have anything to do with this. There was kicking and braying. You talk about a stampede, but John Wayne never saw the likes of it, believe me. We had to stop the loading operations because we were getting nowhere. It was not our problem. We just operated the cargo gear to actually hoist them on board. We had no say in how they were to be slung.

After big discussions amongst the experts, it was decided that they would blindfold the mules and lead them in batches of twenty down to the nets. Now the nets were cargo nets. Pretty hefty things. They would lead the twenty mules right to the centre of the net. Standing around the perimeter of the net were the soldiers. They used to pick up ends and throw them on to the derrick hook. We would pick up the slack and lift the mules up into the air. Well, all you could see was heads sticking out of the sling, tails sticking out, legs sticking out and the bawls and roars of the poor old mules. Mind you I did not blame them. That worked very successfully. We had a thousand mules on board in about six hours. We got them into their pens and they settled down very well indeed. You know, to this day, I am a great admirer of the mules. They are a very, very sensible animal. They accepted their conditions. I think they were only interested in one thing, as long as they were fed and watered they didn't care where they were.

ASKARIS AFFECTIONATELY LOOKED AFTER THE MULES

If any of us went near the mules they would kick out at us but the men looking after them named Askaris, were black people from South Africa. They were very good with animals. They looked after the mules in the pens. They were mucked out regularly, fed and watered. You name it those mules had it.

The Askaris were very good at their job. When we went down on inspection they were sleeping underneath the hooves of the mules. There was never a mule stepped on any of them. They were fond of the animals, sometimes sleeping with their arms around them. It was nice to see the affection they had for the animals.

During the air raids at sea when we would be using our anti-aircraft guns there was noise all over the place, lots of fireworks going on and Germans often bombing us, but it did not seem to bother the mules one little bit. Even though the whole ship shook the mules remained calm. I must hand it to the mule. I have admired them ever since.

During the voyage when we were carrying the mules a very small percentage of the animals would die for one reason or another. We were very successful. I would say we got about ninety eight percent of the animals to the destination but two per cent used to die.

HORSES

We also transported forty to fifty horses called chargers. They were usually for the top brass in the Army. They were used on ceremonial occasions like entering captured towns and cities as they advanced up Italy. They were never used in battle.

The comparison between the mule and those thoroughbred horses was very obvious. Although the mules were calm, not so the horses. They were always very nervous. The old mules, as I said, took it in their stride but the horses kicked their stable doors to pieces. When there were air raids they panicked. Some injured themselves so much they had to be killed.

MULES AND HORSES EATEN

The mules and horses were eaten by the askaris. They used to skin them, butcher and eat them. They asked permission to build brick bases on deck and lit a fire. They put a tub of hot water on the fire and cooked the meat over it. After cooking the meat, they made soup. They always tried to get us to eat some saying, "Would you like some of the mule" Of course, our answer was always, "No thanks." Apparently the best or the most eatable part was the mule's liver. Well, I took their word for it. I certainly was not going to try it.

THE MULES IN THE BATTLE OF MONTE CASINO

The Battle of Monte Casino lasted for months and months. I believe the mules did great work. They used to carry supplies especially around Monte Casino, where the Germans had dug themselves in high mountainous country. They fought a very gallant rear guard delaying action and stopped the allies advance of the Italian peninsular for months. That part of the world wasn't good tank country. It did not lend itself too much to motor transport or tank warfare. It was done the hard way by the poor old footsloggers. Well, to get the supplies up to them the only thing that was any use up there was the mules.

BARI

On one occasion, in between carrying the mules, we loaded a cargo of wounded mules at Bari. They had been up the line and been shot and damaged by shell fire or gun fire. It was most pathetic to see those poor brutes come back down to the ship with massive big bandages wrapped around their heads, around their bellies, around their legs. You know they were unperturbed. They took it all calmly. They were taken to the island in the Mediterranean called Ajaccio, where they had a mule hospital and they were allowed to build up their strength again. They spent months recuperating then the same mules were picked up and taken back to be shot at and killed no doubt. The Company in charge of the mules took them up to the mountain camp.

We eventually took them around the coast to the west side of Italy to Sardinia, where there was a mule hospital, or animal hospital as they called it but it was mainly for mules. We off loaded them at Sardinia and they went into hospital there. By the way we eventually came back, months afterwards, collected the same mules and took them back and they again went into action at Bari.

THE WELL WASHED SHAVING MUG

It was not all bombing and fighting and carrying on there. We did have some good times.

The Army people that we transported on the ship used to endeavour to return the hospitality we had shown them while they were with us. On several occasions we were invited ashore to their transit camps where they were prior to moving up the line.

An Army Officer was a passenger on the ship. We had taken him and his soldiers from Beirut to Bari and we landed them in Bari, sent down a jeep for myself and one or two of the other Officers to have a few drinks with him. We got to the transit camp – they were on the canvas out in the open. We went into the Officers' Mess which was a fairly large tent and we were entertained there. There was plenty of whisky flying around. The only trouble was there was nothing much in which to drink it from. There didn't seem to be any glasses or anything like that. I was given a tin mug and told, "Use that for your whisky. It's my shaving mug but don't worry it's well washed out."

Everything was pretty rough. They lived tough those fellows, believe me. That is the way life was.

We used to hair around in the jeep too. I was asked, "Would you like to go as far as the German main lines?" which was where the fighting was going on. I said, "I don't mind but not too bloody far. I do not want to be getting involved." He replied, "No fear of that. You will hear them before you see them." He was right on that. You could see all the banging and shooting and the tracers flying all over the place long before we got within range of them. We could hear the guns firing further up the hill. "You don't want to go in the direction of the gun fire," which was the German main line, where the fighting was going on. I said I had no intention of doing that. It was an experience.

SICILY

We set sail from Beirut and things were quiet. We had to keep on the coast. Go down as far as Port Said, along the North African coast and then straight across to Sicily. It was as we approached Sicily that the Germans began to take interest in us. I mentioned the Germans all the while. I have never really had much experience of the Italians. I never saw much of them as a fighting force. It was the Germans we had to contend with.

We used to go to Sicily and anchor there. A special convoy used to form up with extra escorts and a lot of anti-aircraft units used to join us there. We would set off and go around the Adriatic and up the coast as far as Bari. Bari was the main Eighth Army base at the time and it was very open to the Germans because the Germans were in Corfu and all up the Yugoslav coast. They had air bases all along there and they could give a lot of attention to anything that moved in the Adriatic.

We set off up the Adriatic. We had to contend with the German Air Force and the German Navy in the shape of E boats and the inevitable mines. There were mine fields all over the place. We used to have the mine sweepers operating ahead of the convoy as we moved along. They used to sweep a channel for us to go through because as soon as the convoy had passed, the Germans would be over again and would relay more mines. I bet there are mines there to this day.

We used to take an awful pasting going up there. There were quite a few ships lost on every passage. It was bloody hard going until you got to Bari. You got rest there because Bari was perpetually under fire from the German bombers. They were over pretty well all the while.

It was the main port, the main supply base of the Eighth Army and it was one of the most vital targets that the Germans had. They were very interested in knocking it out. They very nearly did. There were fourteen ships sunk.

There was one occasion the Germans blew the break water up - put a large breach in it. The Naval Authorities had to take two Merchant ships and sink them right in the entrance in the way of the hole so they could keep on using the Port. It worked very successfully but it was a shame to see two fine ships being used for that purpose, especially when there were all kinds of wrecks all over the place but, of course, they could not move them.

CIVITAVECCHIA

I remember on another occasion we were on the West Coast of Italy. We went into a port called Civitavecchia. It is the nearest port to Rome itself. They referred to it as the Port of Rome. We went in there about twenty -four hours after the Germans moved out. The Yanks had just gone over. They had carpet bombed the place. We moved in with a load of mules and transport. When we moved in I thought, Christ there is no way we are going to get alongside here anywhere. Everything was a shambles, wrecked. You could not see any sign of a wharf. There was a ship in there which had been sunk alongside the wharf. We landed alongside this ship and ran gangways over her. We were able to get mules off using those gangways.

Again, I was invited ashore by some of the people from the mule company. They said, "You will have to use a mule as transport because it is pretty dangerous. There are all kinds of booby traps and mines that the Germans have just scattered all over the place. Some of our fellas have, unfortunately, been killed by them but your best bet is to ride a mule." So, no saddle, just a bridle on the mule. I must say that old animal behaved wonderfully. I had no problems with them and I am certainly no horseman but I went ashore.

I had never seen anything like it. The place was absolutely levelled. There were some lovely buildings in that place, or used to be, and they were just torn wide open. You could see they must have been the homes of people with lots of money because you could see the remains of the furniture, even oil paintings still hanging on the walls and things like that. There was no such thing as Streets. Bulldozers had been through and just cut holes through the rubble. That is where we were plodding along on the mules, looking at the absolute havoc that had been created by the Americans when they carry out this carpet bombing. There used to be a saying that when the Americans came over to bomb the front lines everybody took cover (laugh). The Germans took cover. The British took cover. They used to bomb every damn thing.

They certainly made a mess of Civitaveccia.

When we got back to harbour there was all kind of small craft lying around. Some were in fairly good repair. They were still usable. We located a small yacht that was pretty serviceable and towed it back to the ship behind our lifeboat and took it on board. I do not know what the morals of the thing were but I do not suppose anybody would ever have claimed it anyway.

SARDINIA PRISONERS OF WAR

Our next cargo was a human cargo of Italian prisoners of war. There was a big prisoner of war camp on Sardinia. There were mostly Italians, with a sprinkling of Germans amongst them. Now we had to take about five thousand of those fellas on to the ship to take them back to the Italian mainland.

The Germans were imprisoned but the Italians were disbanded because they were of no threat to anybody. The prisoners we took then most of them were in poor shape. Some had been wounded, some were dying. We had orders to take only people that were reasonably fit. It was heart-breaking to have to stop fellas at the gangway that were obviously on their last legs and would not have survived the journey.

One party of Italian prisoners came down. They had a stretcher and on this stretcher was supposed to be a sick man. He had a blanket over his face. I was at the bottom of the gangway receiving this lot, just checking them on board, numbering them. I had a look at this fella and he was dead! You know they were trying to get him back to the mainland to be buried in his own part of the country. They did not have a hope. We could not take him anyway.

We took five thousand. They had their own rations. We did not feed them. It did not take us long to get back to the mainland. We had them back in I would say twenty- four hours. They left the ship and we resumed our mule carrying. You know that was a picture of the aftermath of war to see those men. I suppose once upon a time they were all proud young men in their uniforms and fancy get up. But to see them now.

They were absolutely defeated. I have never seen a bunch of men so dispirited and so absolutely useless. We were glad to see the back of them because we were not too happy having them on board on account of hygiene problems and disease.

BURMA

On one occasion during our mule carrying period, we were side tracked for a couple of months. We were sent out of the Mediterranean. We loaded up with stores in Port Said and Suez. It was again mainly the war time stuff, you know, armaments and bombs and army rations. We loaded up this lot still with all our mule carrying equipment on board. This was a rush job. We were going back to carrying the mules anyway when we had finished.

We were side tracked out of the Mediterranean and went down to Chittagong. Our supplies were for Windgate and the Chindits, who were then beginning to make themselves felt in Burma and around that area. They were beginning to push the Japanese down the peninsular, down towards Singapore again. Chittagong was, of course, our main base and we landed all our stores there. We did not see anything.

That was a rest period as far as I was concerned. There were no problems. If you could enjoy the war time, well, I enjoyed that period because in Chittagong there were quite a lot of social activities going on. We had a good time there. The irony of that was we did not see any activity but every member of the ship's crew was subsequently awarded the Burma Star for just being in Chittagong.

ALL THINGS COME TO AN END

We eventually came back and resumed our mule carrying. I must have been about eighteen months on that job in the Mediterranean. I thought we were never going to get out of it. But all in all, things come to an end sooner or later, good or bad.

We were having trouble with the boilers. They were on their last legs. It was decided to send us out of the Mediterranean. They took us into Alexandria and dismantled all our mule carrying equipment. We loaded lots of army stuff again. We were loading tanks and ammunitions, you name it, and we were taking them back out again from Alexandria.

Things had quietened down in North Africa. There were only Army garrisons there now. The Germans and all the rest of them were long gone. They were fighting up the Italian mainland so there was no longer any need for all this weaponry and stuff in the Middle East or in North Africa. So, we loaded all this stuff up and took it back to the U.K. I suppose some of it was subsequently used on D Day at the landing at Normandy. But that was it. We got back to the U.K. and paid off.

CHIEF OFFICER

I didn't actually leave the ship on that occasion. I had some leave. I did not go back to Wexford. I did not have time for that. I had a few weeks leave which I spent with my lady friend in Liverpool and thoroughly enjoyed it but I was back on the Anglo African again.

I think I had forgotten to mention that while we had been carrying the mules our Chief Officer had come down ill and had been landed at the British Hospital in Port Said. The remaining Officers were just stepped up one position. I went from Second Officer to Chief Officer and the Second Mate likewise. The Senior Apprentice became Third Mate. When I resigned from the Anglo African after coming back from the mule run, I still retained the position as Chief Officer. In fact, I was never again Second Officer. I retained that position until I got my Master's Certificate.

ALLIED LANDING IN SOUTH OF FRANCE

We took war stores back down to the Mediterranean again. We were a supply ship for part of the landing that took part in the south of France. I was not at the D-Day landing but I did take a small part in the landing on the south of France, which did not get much publicity. It was very very successful because they out flanked the Germans badly in Italy and they had to pull back faster than they would have had to. It tied up a hell of a lot of the German Army. The landing in the south of France. The Army did not advance too far in France - a holding operation just to tie up large portions of the German Army.

Whilst this war was going on the D-Day preparations were in full swing and of course the landing on the Normandy beaches subsequently took place and that was more or less the end of the war. Well, not quite I suppose but you could see the end of the war then.

The Germans put up a hell of a tough fight from there on. The Allied forces had to fight for every flipping inch of the country all the way damn near to Berlin. When you think that the Russians were on the other side pounding the German Army, it amazed me that they held out so long. I was always full of admiration for them, regardless of the ideology behind the German Army. They certainly were a far superior army to anything that we had on our side.

The Germans, I would say, were beaten by numbers and by American production. As I said, they fought all the way back to Berlin and that was the end of it. That was more or less the end of the war for me, the actual fighting war anyway. Well not quite actually.

WAR'S END, STILL THE U BOATS

I was Chief Officer of the Anglo African for quite some time. We had a trip across to Montreal where we loaded grain for the U.K. The U boats were still fairly active across the North Atlantic. They were still managing to sink the ships. They did not have any problems. After we discharged the grain, we set sail again and this time we went to Boston and loaded a cargo of timber. We were in Boston for about three weeks. The Yanks were very good to us. They certainly treated us very well.

I had a cousin there, Eileen Kineally. She was a daughter of my father's sister, Aunty Eassie. She was a nurse. She was married and lived in and around Boston. I saw her there. We had several nights out at her home. She was very good to us.

ONLY A MATTER OF TIME

We loaded timber there and it took us quite some time. After we finished the loading, it was back up to Halifax to queue up for a convoy. It looked now as if the Germans were on their last legs and they were expecting the capitulation any time. They were in Berlin now. The Russians had reached Berlin and the Yanks and the British were on the other side of it. They were just pounding the place to bits. They had no other option but surrender. I think Hitler by this time had topped himself. It was only a matter of time before the Germans packed in.

UPROAR

When we left Halifax in convoy the war was still on and the U boats, strange to say, were still active but not so active as they had been I suppose. They saw the writing on the wall too and they were keeping their heads down. We were about five or six days out of Halifax when we got the word that the German war was over and all remaining U boats had been accounted for. They had identified themselves and were on the surface. The orders were then that all shipping to proceed independently. There was great uproar in the convoy. There were guns shooting up in the air and firing up rockets and all kinds of things. Everybody was delighted of course that the German war was over. The Japanese were still fighting away out in the East. They were not doing so good either.

PEACE

I did not get involved too much with the Japanese war, except that I had been in Singapore not too long before Singapore fell and we evacuated quite a few people from Singapore. That was my only involvement with the Japanese side of it.

We proceeded independently then. Believe me it was a great feeling of relief to be able to go your own gait and do what you wanted to do yourself. You were not stuck in a convoy and you were not watching the Commodore hoist up signals telling you to alter course so many degrees to starboard or so many degrees to port. It was nice to be on our own again and knowing now that you were quite safe. We got back to the U.K. and I left the Anglo African.

It was a very happy time for people that had come through the war relatively unscathed. Everybody I knew in the immediate vicinity of where I was staying around September Road in Liverpool and the few fellas that I used to knock around with, they all came through ok so we were all very happy about it. September Road itself was not touched. The only thing that happened to September Road was that some of the roofs were damaged by anti- aircraft bits and pieces coming down. The firing of shells up on the air and bits of the shrapnel would just fall back down again. That cracked the tiles on the roofs where they struck. That was the only thing that happened in September Road.

The fellas who went through the war, fought in the war, they were just discarded. The English were the world's worst. As soon as they used you in the war and the war was over, they did not want to know you anymore. You were an expense. They did not get any medical attention. They lost a leg and until it healed you were on your own. They made their own wooden stumps and crutches. They sat in Church Street in the cold all day long selling matches. You could not just sit without selling something. Some people just gave them the money without buying the matches. There were a lot of people who never got the honour they deserved. They should have got some recognition. They were the ones who should have got the medals.

I did not think much of Churchill. He was arrogant. He got the kudos. He inspired people without doubt but he also inspired himself.

England now is a very civilised country. You cannot beat it. I have been all over the world and never seen such a great country as England. Maybe Ireland basing themselves on England. In 1948 we began our National Health Service. Nothing like it throughout the world. We look after our sick people free of charge. We have got the best service in the world here and we don't know it.

To think everybody, including myself, stepped over dead bodies lying in the main Street of Calcutta. It was noted for it. Poor souls just go so far and they pack up and collapse. We get up of a morning and have our breakfast. They get up and have to steal it or starve, as they have no way of earning. If you are a sick person in the United States, you are in trouble. You will not be looked at unless they see your Bank card to see whether you can pay for their services. The Health Service in the States exploit the people they should be looking after. You certainly would need a big Insurance if you lived there. A lot of Doctors in the States are rich men. I did not really like their attitude, you know.

They thought there was no place like America.

NAGASAKI

I was in Japan about three months after the atomic bomb had been dropped. I was in parts of Japan. I was in Osaka, Kobe and Nagasaki. That was down where the bomb was dropped. This was three months after that bomb had done all that damage. When we got there it was still more or less the same as it was after the bomb had been dropped. There were no restrictions about going ashore or anything like that. Nobody said anything about radioactivity We used to wander around this devastated town of Nagasaki. It was a hell of a sight.

It really was awesome to think that one single bomb could do such damage to a big city. It left a hell of an impression on me. I said, "Bloody hell if there is another war and they use those things there won't be much hope for us."

I remember thinking then the Japanese were down and out. They had nothing. No industry. Their shipping was non-existent. There was no work. They were hungry. They were everything. We used to discharge there. I think it was salt and grain. The Japs were damn glad to see us then. I remember when we berthed all the remains of factories, industries, as it was before they were bombed, they were all in ruins.

The Japanese work force was trying to tear up the damage. They were doing this mostly the hard way, with no equipment. I remember the young fellas before they started work in the morning they used to form up in any spare clean or clear ground that they could find and go through their exercises. Limbering up, physical jerks, the lot of it. I said to myself "Christ those fellas. It will not be long before they are back on their feet again."

I have no liking for them but I have to admire them for the way they recovered. I was never surprised at the way they did come back. The power that they have now in the world. It really frightens me to think that they really more or less commercially rule the world. As I said you have to admire them for it.

1946 – 1966 MASTER MARINER

I resumed my studies for my Master's Certificate, which put me into 1946. I think I went to College around about May 1946. Again, I gave myself three months to polish up my records and so forth. I was quite lucky. I took the examination and did not have to go back a second time. Went through the first time so I had my Certificate then. After I got the results down at the Board of Trade, as it was called in those days, I 'phoned my good lady. She worked then. She worked for a firm of jewellers in Liverpool called Alfred Wolfe. I told her the good news and arranged to take her out to dinner. We had a very good evening.

MARRIED MAN

I think I finally got my Master's Certificate in July 1946 so Babe and I arranged to get married on 3rd August 1946. I must say you know we all say the same thing about our wives but it was the best day's work I ever did. All through my married life I never had any cause to complain whatsoever. I have always had a very happy life. As far as Babe was concerned, I came first and as far as I was concerned Babe came first. Now just do not get the idea that we didn't have a good bust up now and then. We had a good fight but they never lasted. It was just an ordinary run of the bloody affair thing. Half the time you could not remember what you were fighting about. When I married Babe, they were not too keen on it in Wexford. She got a cool reception, and I took a dim view of it. I knew what I wanted and never had any regrets. She became a blue eye with them eventually.

It was a good move on my part when I married Babe. She was a hell of a nice girl. She certainly did a lot for me. As I said, I used to make long voyages in those days and when I came back from a voyage everything had been paid up. There were no debts to face. She took charge of everything. I never had to worry about bills being paid. She was a damn good hand at looking after the accounts. I could go on for a long time telling you about what a wonderful married life I had but it is the case.

Anyway, we got married and had a very nice reception. In those days things were still pretty scarce. Everyone was on rations. You had to have coupons for this and coupons for the other thing. Her mother, God be good to her, did us proud. We had plenty to eat and plenty to drink.

HONEYMOON

Babe and I took off on our honeymoon in the afternoon. We left them all to it and went down to Lime Street station. I was married in uniform. I did not want to be married in uniform. I preferred civies. I gave in to popular demand. In those days it paid you to travel in uniform because anybody with any war connection with the armed forces and all the rest always got priority as regards travel. We went to Harlow for our honeymoon. That was where Babe did most of her time in the Land Army and I used to go down and see her in Harlow. In fact, I think that was where we finally made up our minds to marry.

We got down to Lime Street Station. The trains were packed in those days but one of the guards I remember realised that we were a newly married couple and gave us a compartment right on the end of a carriage. In those days they were very small compartments that used to be tucked on the end of a carriage. There were only seats on one side. He said, "Get in there now and I will lock the door and you won't be troubled all the way to Euston Station." He was right. We had it all to ourselves all the way. We often think about that. It was a very nice thought.

We changed trains at Euston Station and eventually got to Harlow where the people that Babe used to stay with had arranged to put us up. The food was on ration. You would not get anything in a Hotel in regard to food. Harlow was a kind of country town in those days. The people Babe knew were the salt of the earth. They put us up and made a fuss of us. We had a very very nice honeymoon believe me. It was beautiful country down there. Some lovely real old-fashioned pubs, hundreds of years old. We used to call in of an evening after a stroll. There used to be singsongs. Everybody was in a happy mood. The war was over. The fellas had come back from the various fighting fronts and things were getting back to normal again.

After our honeymoon was over, we came back to September Road. We had no home of our own then. We lived with Babe's people and it was a very happy arrangement. It suited me because I did not like the idea of leaving Babe in a house on her own, even if I could have afforded to have bought a house in those days, which I could not. They gave us the main room of the house which was the front room. We had a bed, which was a very important piece of equipment. We had a settee and a few armchairs. We had a radio. That was the sum total of our possessions but we were as happy as Larry. We really enjoyed life. The only fly in the ointment was that I had to go back to sea. Unfortunately, within a couple of weeks I was called back.

BRADFORD CITY

I think my next ship was Bradford City. It was when we parted Babe came down with me and was on the ship. I think the ship was in Avonmouth if I remember rightly. She was discharging down there and doing some repairs before she finally sailed again. It was a tough time, believe me. Neither of us liked the idea of being parted again but there was nothing for it but to go.

We took a cargo of coal out to Halifax. I was again Chief Officer. We discharged all cargo at Halifax without any problems. We then had to go down to Port Said, which is only about twenty-four hours away sailing time, to load salt for Japan.

SALT AND PORT SAID

After discharging the coal when you took a salt cargo on board you had to whitewash your holds out. It was quite a job getting the ship ready. The way we did the whitewashing job was we just used the sprayers and sprayed everything. We just left the coal dust in the holds and just prayed over and it came up nice and white. By the time we go to Port Said, which was working around the clock, we had the ship ready to load salt. We tied up at the berth at Port Said and started to load salt. It used to be a very slow job in those days. It was done by fellas carrying baskets up planks and just dumping it into the various holds. Talk about a chain gang. It used to be a continuous stream of human beings up one plank and down another plank. It was just a continuous, endless belt of baskets of salt. It took a long time. Of course, there was no work at night.

REPELLING BOARDERS – NO SUCH THING AS LAW

In those days at Port Said and Alex there was no such thing as law. It was just after the war and there was a hell of a lot of bad eggs about. I mean Egyptians. Going ashore in Port Said you took your life in your flipping hands. Gangs of thieves and thugs used to raid the ships of a night. They used to climb up the moorings. The gangway was always guarded but they were like monkeys, they could climb up the ropes. They were into your accommodation before you knew anything and they were vicious buggers. They were quite capable of using a knife. Well, we had plenty of good warning of this so we posted night gangs. They used to come up over the stern. We would have a bunch of fellas on the deck. We would be behind stores or anything we could find and lay doggo and wait for them to start climbing the ropes. As soon as they got near the rails we would up with sticks and all kinds of things and beat the hell out of them. They used to fall off the rope and into the water. We kept it up and had no problems. They certainly did not get aboard anyway. There were many ships there that had not taken precautions. Lots of people got injured you know. There was one or two fatalities. It paid you to keep things in hand. We were glad to get out of there.

STOWAWAYS

We sailed and went down through the canal out into the Suez and down the Red Sea to Aden. We took bunkers at Aden. We were only in there for about six hours. We sailed and were a few hours at sea when three strange faces suddenly appeared on deck. We realised we had three stowaways. Now in those days if you had stowaways, you could not land them in any country. Most of them were probably refugees but they had no papers to identify them. You did not know where they came from or anything about them. There was a consultation with the Captain, and it was decided that we just had to land them on the Somali coast. Not in any port. They said they were Somalis, so, as Somalia was just right opposite Aden we crossed over to the Somali coast. During the night we made a good heavy raft and put stocks of water and food on it.

The following morning when dawn broke the coastline was there so we steamed in on the lead. Got in as close as we possible could. We got about half a mile off the coast when we put the raft over the side and ordered the stowaways on to it. We pointed to the coast and said "Somali." We left them to it, and we backed off.

You know I was a young fella in those days and I did not think much of it but you know in latter years I have given that a lot of thought. I wonder what happened to those poor buggers because it was a very inhospitable coast. There was a lighthouse close to where we landed them and I am sure they made their way there. There was a hell of a lot of lawlessness in those days you know. Piracy was rearing its ugly head. Not so much with Merchant ships but amongst the coastal traffic. The dhows and all this kind of stuff. The people on those ships were fair game. I was just wondering if the fellas we put on the raft got foul of that crowd and I hope the hell they did not.

I had a bit of a guilty conscience about that later but I suppose it was not really my responsibility to land them. It was the Captain's responsibility. I could have objected but in fact I do not think I objected at all. Once you got them on the ship you were going to have a hell of a job trying to get them off. Every port, in every country you went to, they had to be taken ashore and incarcerated in the local jail under armed guard until the ship sailed again. Then they would have been put back on the ship and that would have been an expensive proposition. I do not think the owners would have been too pleased. That was the story of the stowaways. We never heard any more about it.

HOME AGAIN

We carried on to Japan and discharged our cargo of salt and subsequently sailed off across to Vancouver, British Columbia to load grain. Of course, you had to get the ship ready to load grain up, putting up all kinds of fixings on the ship itself. It is quite an involved job. I will not go into it but you did all things yourselves in those days. By the time we got to Vancouver we were ready to load grain back to Avonmouth. Again, no problems. Just the ordinary run of the mill voyage. Babe was there on the dock side to meet me when I arrived. It was a great reunion and we had a great time.

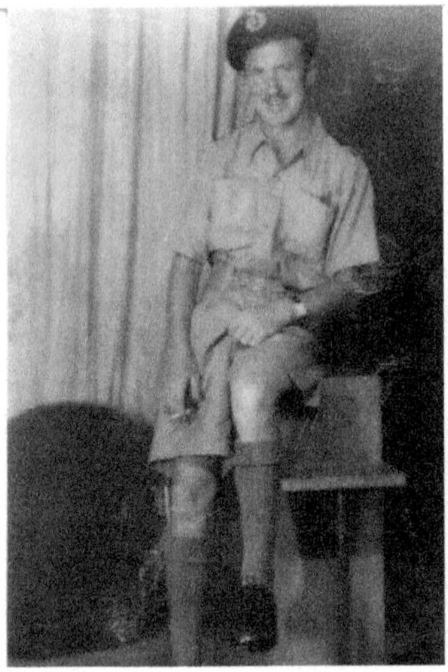

1951

Mark
having
d the
Navy.

Commodore Mark Higgins (left) on the occasion of his retirement from the Reardon Smith Shipping Line.

Mark serving on the MV Bradford City in 1947 loading cargo in Egypt for Japan.

Commodore Higgins and his wife Ann

'om Thomas Street
an MBE in 100 years

TITANIC

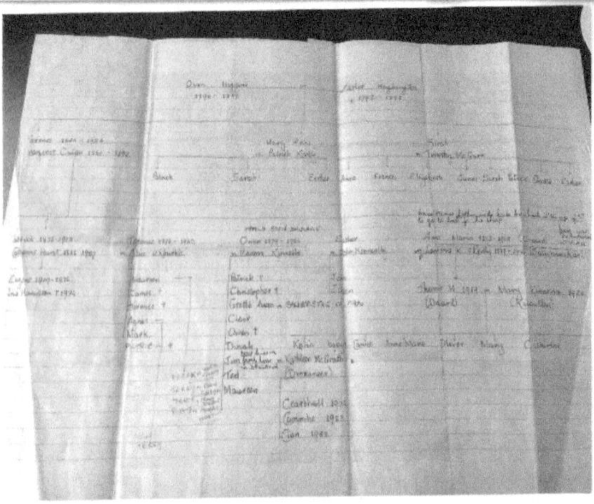
Patrick †
Christopher †
Clare
Owen †
Mark
Ted
Maureen

FIRST COMMAND

I did not leave the ship. The Captain left and another Captain joined who I had been shipmates with before on the Sacramento Valley. He was the fella who used to keep his mosquito door in the apprentice's bunk on this particular ship and I fell out with him over that. At least he took exception to me chucking the ruddy old door out and I, of course, had a tough voyage then. He joined as Captain and I was Chief Officer. I had more power to my arm then. I expected it was going to be a miserable bloody voyage again but he was a changed man. He was not too well, and we got on very well together. We had quite a pleasant voyage. In fact, we used to reminisce about the voyage on the Sacramento Valley. He laughed about it. I said, "I wasn't bloody laughing when I had you and a bloody old skipper breathing down my neck every five minutes." He said, "Let bygones be bygones."

Before we reached Vancouver the Captain had become ill. I assumed it was heart trouble because he had all the symptoms of it. We did our best for him. I landed him at Vancouver when we got there. The sum total of it was that he would not be able to sail in the ship when she completed loading as he more or less needed intensive care for quite some time.

I had to cable the owners about all this. Communications were still pretty primitive in those days. You did everything by cable. Flying and things like that was not as prevalent as it is now. There was no way they could get a relief Captain out there, so they told me to take the ship over and bring it back to London which I did. That was my first command. I was twenty- eight and to be faced with this bloody thing of taking the ship back, even though you had a certificate as a Master Mariner, it is a different thing having to actually do the job at short notice. It went off alright. There were no great problems. We eventually got to London and it was at London that I said I had enough now. After that lot I want a holiday. I left the ship and went home.

I had a fairly good leave. I think about three months. I really enjoyed it. We went to Wexford and saw the folks there. Everybody was very pleased to see us. We went down to Babe's family home in Herrylock Lane, Templetown in the Hook area. Babe's family home is the bottom of Herrylock Lane, Templetown. All her relations were unfortunately dead and we stayed with friends.

Babe was christened Anastasia as was our daughter, but at the Hook the name on a new born was often given Baby and so it became shortened to Babe all her life and our daughter Anastasia we always called Babs. Babe had a sister Mary and she was always known as Babsy. That is how it was in the Hook area.

We stayed with a couple at the top Herrylock Lane, Mary Kate and Simon Connolly. A great pair. Simon would have made a fortune as a comedian. He used to tell some great stories. He told them in a very natural everyday conversation type. Their house is the only original one still in the Lane. A lovely modern home is where the second old house was and sadly Babe's home now has only one ivy covered wall standing. We returned to Liverpool after quite some time in Ireland and took up living with Babe's Mum and Dad. Just normal life then. We did not look for a home of our own. Babe's parents persuaded her that it would be best to stay with them for a few years anyway until we were on our feet. We had no objection to it. It was a very nice arrangement. As I said before, they were very nice people. We had some great times together. One of the things that influenced me was Mrs. Gray, who was Babe's mother. May, I shall refer to her as. She was a hell of a great cook. Boy, she looked after us. We had a very pleasant time then the two of us. We spent most of it out, travelling around the country. We did not have a car in those days but we got around quite a bit. We had a lot of free time and we were able to enjoy ourselves. But all good things come to an end and before too long the dreaded day of having to go back to sea again arrived.

GREAT CITY

I went down to Cardiff and joined the Great City. Used to be known as the Great Pity. The Captain of that ship was as long as he was broad. A great tough little fella. I think he just about lived on gin. He could drink so much you never knew he had had a drink. He used to certainly get it down him. I do not know how many bottles a day he would get through but it had no apparent effect on him.

FORT CHURCHILL

We set off from Cardiff. We were on a new run this time. Something I had not been on before. We were going up to the Arctic. Past the Arctic Circle up the Hudson Strait into Hudson Bay and eventually arrived at a place called Fort Churchill. That is a port that's only open six weeks of the year and its only export is grain. The grain is shipped in from the Northern Territories of Canada. As I say there is nothing in Fort Churchill but this grain elevator

ICEBERGS

The story about that is there were two ships bound for Fort Churchill at the same time. We were supposed to be the second ship in. There was always a big fuss made of the opening of the port and the first ship in. The Captain was always presented with (used to be) a silver pen and ink stand. The pad of the stand was made from an ox's hoof. It was a very nice thing and, of course, it was quite an honour to be the first ship in. We thought we did not have a chance of getting into Fort Churchill as first ship. We were quite content to go in as second. We entered the Hudson Strait. We had no radar in those days and the Hudson is a great place for icebergs. There are always icebergs in and out of Hudson Strait, especially at the beginning of summer when the sea ice begins to break up and the icebergs are able to drift out and down the Hudson Strait and out into the North Atlantic.

FIRST IN WRONG SHIP

We entered the Hudson Strait. We could see the icebergs in daylight but when it became dark you could not see anything. We had to stop and stay where we were and wait until the following morning before you could see because you drifted at the same speed as the icebergs. It was to avoid the possibility of running into one. So, daylight again, we picked up and felt our way through the ice. This is broken ice now and eventually arrived off Fort Churchill. The pilot came out and took us in. Eventually we tied up. There was great consternation. We were the wrong ship! The ship they were expecting in as first ship had not materialised. Apparently, she was dodging icebergs. I believe she had radar too so there was no reason she should not have got in. Anyway, there had been arrangements for the reception to be held on this ship. There was a party and all this kind of stuff. So, they hurriedly changed all this and the reception was held on the Great City.

THE VICEROY OF CANADA – THE BIG SHOT

Viscount Lord Alexander, the Viceroy of Canada at the time, was in Fort Churchill. He was the overall Commander of the Eighth Army at the time of the Battle of Alamein. He was superior to Montgomery but that is beside the point. He was the man that would make the presentations to the Captain of the ship. We were hurriedly advised about this. We had started to load grain again and, of course, I was dressed up in my working gear. I was looking after the ship, putting the grain aboard. I was still Chief Officer of course.

An official came down from the Port Authority and told me that this big shot and his entourage would board the ship at two o'clock in the afternoon and would make the presentation to the Captain of the ship. Well, it was damn near that time when I was told. I ran up and told the old Skipper "There is a crowd coming down to present you with some kind of memento for being the first ship into the port for the season. He had been lying down and I remember him saying, "Bloody hell they could have waited until I got my sleep in." Between 1pm and 3pm is sacrosanct as regards to sleep, especially at sea of course but the Old Man he used to have his sleep at sea and in port. He hurriedly arose from his bed. Got himself cleaned up and managed to find a uniform of some description and had the stewards lined up to do the necessary.

The cavalcade arrived down at the gangway. I was the reception committee. I had the honour of meeting this Field Marshall Viscount Lord Alexander on the gangway. I was dressed in a rather scruffy old boiler suit. I introduced myself. Made myself known to the personage and just told him, "I am sorry this is a working ship and we are loading cargo. I will take you to the Captain." He must have had about fifteen army bods or army type fellas along with him – his entourage. I suppose his staff. I took him up to the Captain's quarters and, of course, they all came along into the Captain's room. I could see the look on the Old Man's face when all this crew crowded into his room. "Christ," he told me afterwards he had said to himself. "How the hell am I going to look after all this lot? They will drink me out of house and home."

VISCOUNT GROUSE SHOOTING

Well, it was a very pleasant do. I was not there but the Old Man told me about it afterwards. He said they drank quite a lot of whisky. Alexander did not drink much but his staff did and they enjoyed themselves. Alexander made a bit of a speech and welcomed the Captain into the port and made his presentation.

Then he told the Captain, "I'm up here to inspect the radar installations. There used to be radar installations up there then keeping an eye on the Russians on the other side of the Pole. That is what I am up here doing but I am taking the opportunity to do some shooting up here. It is great country for pheasant and grouse. Grouse more than anything else." The Old Man, bold as brass, said, "Well if you have any luck, I wouldn't mind a brace or two." Alexander said, "I will remember that Captain." That was the end of the party.

I remember Alexander came down on deck and I was taking him to the gangway and he said to me, "Chief Officer I would like to go round and just look at the loading to see how it is done." So, I took him to one of the hatches that was loading grain and explained to him how it was done and all the rest of it. He was very nice and thanked me profusely and took his departure. We said to ourselves, "Well that is the end of that. We will not see any more of him." We continued our loading. To conclude the story, a few days later one of the Army types came back down to the ship and lo and behold he had a double brace of grouse for the Skipper. He kept his word.

Fort Churchill was a very very primitive place. There was a Hudson Bay trading store there. It was just what you would imagine if you read about the fur trappers and their way of life. It seems that they used to come into the Hudson Bay store with their catch, which would be furs. They used to go out into the wilderness and trap their game over a period of three to four months. When they came back to Churchill they were just like ruddy mad men. They used to sell of their catch of furs to the Hudson Bay. Take cash, supplies, booze and they used to be bloody mad. You were not safe when them fellas were around. Talk about the mountain men. They were really tough fellas.

The Captain of the ship got in touch with one of them before he had disposed of his furs. He was interested in buying some of the skins to take home and have made into a cape for his wife. So, he met this fella and he let him have a very rare pelt. I think several pelts. I think it was what they called the white fox, or the silver fox, I am not quite sure now. The Skipper was delighted to get this and all the payment he asked for was a gallon of navy rum, which we had plenty of on board! The Old Man was very pleased to make the bargain.

SHED NO TEARS

We eventually sailed out of Churchill and came back to the Humber and discharged our cargo there. It was a quick turn around and before we knew where we were, we were on our way back to Churchill to take a second cargo out of the port. We just managed to get into Fort Churchill again for the second time, load our cargo of wheat and take it out. Even then the ice was coming down the river. The ice was beginning to form. The blizzards were beginning to start. Churchill is a place where the wind never stops blowing. It is the most desolate bloody hole I have ever been to. Believe me I was glad to see the back end of it. I was never back there again and (chuckle) I shed no tears about it.

THE NEAR CENTRE OF A HURRICANE - AN EVIL PLACE TO BE

Normally the near centre of the hurricane hits the Florida Straights and travels up the east coast of the U.S.A. roughly as far as New York, where it recurves and heads out into the North Atlantic in a north easterly direction, easing down all the while. The British Isles sometimes gets the tail end of a hurricane with winds roughly fifty to sixty miles an hour. Hurricanes in the North Atlantic usually start on the equatorial line and they are just small whirl winds. A lot of them just fade away but one or two will develop into a full-scale hurricane and will travel westerly where they start to recurve in a north westerly direction. They follow a well-designed track with a possibility when they hit the West Indies that they could go deeper into the Gulf of Mexico before recurving in a northerly direction.

The West Indies is not a safe place to build houses. August, September to the middle of October is the hurricane season. This is the time to be out of the West Indies.

DAUGHTER BORN

I think after I left the Bradford City I was home again on leave. It was very enjoyable especially when our daughter was born in 1949. That was a big occasion in my life. I should say our lives. I remember I came into Southampton on a ship. We were discharging cargo in Southampton but I managed to get off and travel all the way from Southampton up to Liverpool to see my offspring and, of course, my wife. It was a great moment. She was only a little tiny thing. She was six months old when I first saw her. She was named the same as her mother Anastasia, but as I said previously, we always called her Babs. I was a proud father and all that. It was very nice to have her. We had a great time with her. She made life very interesting.

PARIS CITY RUN AGROUND TORREVIAJA

My next ship, the Paris City, was a wartime-built ship. I think I joined her around about 1950. I was

Chief Officer again. Of course, in those days it was white crews. We did not have any Indian crews prior to then. We set sail in ballast from Cardiff bound for a little Spanish port called Torrevieja on the Mediterranean side, about forty miles south of Alicante. Well, as I think I mentioned before, when you carry salt cargoes you have to whitewash the insides of your hold, which we did on the passage down.

We arrived off Torrevieja and there was no berth available. There was a ship there before us loading salt. We went into the port, anchored inside the break- water and were inspected. Then we had to go out again and anchor about a mile outside the break water. It was only a small port. There was no room for a ship to be at anchor there, she would interfere with traffic. We went out again and anchored. We were in ballast now. A ship in ballast has no cargo. Like a flipping big balloon on top of the water.

MISTRAL

Survived hurricanes and every damn thing yet still managed to run aground twenty miles south of Alicante. During the night one of those sudden storms came down from the Gulf of Lyons. They were called mistrals. They blow at hurricane force winds. They do not last for anything more than twenty-four hours. This one hit us. We were at anchor of course. With the heavy swell the ship being in ballast was pretty well unmanageable.

We had no control over the ship. She started to drag her anchors. We dropped the other anchor down as soon as the wind started to freshen. We had as much cable on them as we possibly could but to no avail. She started to drag them. We tried to get them in to see if we could get out to sea but she would not handle.

Anyway, we eventually hit the first reef. The reefs in the Mediterranean are all covered with kelp. They do not damage so much as a bald reef. What happens is they send the floors up and they buckle the keel plating and all the rest of it. We went over three sets of those reefs before we finally ended up on the beach. We came in on the reef, six foot of kelp, which we slid over, but we could not go out the same way.

PANDEMONIUM

I tell you it was a hectic night. With the ship rolling over on her beam ends and the keel getting on to the reef the next sea would hit her and bang her on to the reef on the other side. You can imagine the pandemonium that was going on. There was not a thing that we could do. Even though we were flying light the sea was coming aboard.

You would think you were in the middle of a western ocean full scale storm. It was all broken water, of course, and it would have been fatal for anybody to be on deck at all. If you went over in that lot, you would not have stood a chance. So, we kept ourselves screwed up in the accommodation. Lots of doors were stoved in and the wing of the bridge went but we eventually rolled over the three reefs and came to a stop. The sea was still hitting us on the seaward side of the ship. The other side was up on the beach.

SHIP ON BEACH

This, of course, all happened at night. You could not see anything and the beach we landed on there was very little habitation. It was mostly country. I remember being on the wing of the bridge with the Old Man, just trying to see where we were. He said to me, "Mark I do not think we are going to go any further tonight. I think we have gone as far as we are going to go." We just went back into the wheelhouse just talking there and the dawn started to break.

You might not believe this but the first signs of human life we saw was a young lad walking along the dunes with a herd of goats. He had come out from the town of Torrevieja. Apparently, they just take the goats out and walk them over any place where they can forage and that was his job for the day and he takes them back at night. He was, of course, several hundred yards away but we had the glasses on him. He did not go behind them. He went ahead of them. He had some kind of a flute he used to play as he went along.

We had sent up distress flares and we had been on the radio but you know the Spaniards they are not too quick to respond to anything. It is manana with them.

We eventually had the Spanish Rescue Service on the beach, or what was purported to be the Spanish Rescue Service. Anyway, we were in. We had no problems then. I mean no dangerous problems. We were high and dry on the beach and the wind had dropped down. As I said it comes suddenly and it goes suddenly. There was a bit of a swell still hitting the weather side of the ship and she was still drawing a lot of spray over but nobody was in any great danger. There was nothing they could do for us and we told them we were ok. They left an armed guard there. What for I do not know but we went down and had our breakfast and let the owners know through cable and it caused consternation then.

GREAT PALAVER

As I said, we took stock of what had happened and decided we were going to be here for a long time. There is no rise and fall of water in the Mediterranean. The sea only rises when it is blown up by a storm but as soon as the win drops the sea goes down.

So, the sea went down and receded and left us more-or-less high and dry on the sand. We were dry on the inside of the ship. On the landward side you could pretty well walk around the outside of the ship. That will give you an idea of how far we were up. Of course, there was nothing that we could do to lighten her because there was very little ballast in her and certainly no cargo in her. We eventually got the gangway down on to the strand and some of the Port authorities came out and there was great palaver going on.

AGROUND SIX MONTHS

In the heel of the hunt, we were there for six months. I would not call it a tragedy, but nobody likes to see a fine ship more or less wrecked. We were about three miles from the town of Torrevieja, the Port where we were going to load salt.

FINEST TIME OF MY SEAFARING LIFE

It was March we went up on the beach. We were there for six months with the weather improving all the while. The sun was getting hotter and there was the finest swimming. The seas around there are absolutely crystal clear. It was absolutely gorgeous. We caused no pollution. Our fuel tanks did not rupture. As I said, the reefs were covered with about two feet of kelp so they did not do any actual puncturing of tanks. We got our lifeboat down eventually and managed to get it in operation. The salvage crowd gouged out a little channel for us so as we could get the lifeboat away from the ship and backward and forward. We used to use the lifeboat to go ashore with initially.

We used to have to go out to sea down the coast a bit, through the breakwater and into the port. We used to have to go there for stores and things like that. There were not too many stores in Spain after the war and it was hard to get anything. People had a pretty tough time there but fortunately Smiths had a big contract to load quite a lot of salt for Japan. Quite a few of the ships were coming to Torrevieja so they used to bring us down stores on the quiet.

The Spanish Customs were the worst bastards I have ever dealt with. To take stores from another ship was nigh on impossible if you went about it legally. What we did was, when one of our ships was in loading salt, to sneak into the port in our lifeboat in the small hours of the night and take stores when all the Spanish authorities were asleep. At least we hoped they were bloody well asleep. Anyway, we were never caught. So, we lived pretty well on the ship.

HONORARY MEMBERS TORREVIEJA LOCAL BUSINESSMEN'S CLUB

The ordinary people of Torrevieja were very, very, nice indeed and they did their best for us.

The power in Spain were the political figures. They ran everything. Unless you kept your nose clean you could have trouble. Myself and the Old Man and Second Mate were made honorary members of the local businessmen's club there. It was like a Rotary Club. It was a very posh place I can assure you. Drink there like gin and Cointreau was like water and the beer was quite good. As honorary members of the club you could eat there. It was about the only place on the whole of Torrevieja to eat anything. As long as you did not drink the water in that part of the world you were alright.

There was very little English spoken there so if you wanted anything or to do anything you more or less had to try and speak Spanish a bit. By the end of the six months, I was not a bad hand at it at all. I could more or less understand what people were saying to me and they could get the gist of what I was saying. It worked out very well and as I said they became very kind to us. I would not mind living in Spain.

THE GRANDEE

The actual place where the ship was on the beach was part of a big vineyard. There were vineyards all at the back of the beach and a big farmhouse, the Villa Blanca I think it was called. It belonged to a Spanish grandee who used it as a summer holiday house. His vineyards were managed and run by the locals. When he heard that we were on his beach he came down from Madrid. He came aboard and made himself known to the Captain. He was a very, very, decent fellow. He could speak English. He said, "Anything we can do to help you we would be only too pleased. I keep a lot of small boats up in the farm and pedal boats – they are all up there. Please use them by all means."

He again warned us about the water. "The water around here you must not drink it unless you have bought it. We do not drink it at all. As you know we drink a lot of wine. I will supply you with wine from my vineyard. It is what we drink with meals normally." It was what they called the rough white and the rough red. It was very very nice stuff. He sent us down as much of that as we could handle. He used to send down demijohns. We must have drunk gallons and gallons and gallons of the stuff. It was great we used to have it for breakfast, for lunch and we had it for dinner. It was very enjoyable. He said, "There are bicycles up there you can use when you want to go from the ship to the town."

NOBODY CAME TO ANY GRIEF

The roads in Spain, especially in that part of the world, were the world's worst and there were no lights. It would probably be light when you went into town but coming back in the small hours of the morning it would be pitch black. They used to bring farm produce into the town on bullocks and carts. No lights on them whatsoever. You would be riding back out of the town and you would be quite happy of course. You would be full of Cointreau and stuff like that and the next minute you would end up, chuckle, crashing into a bloody bullock. You would not even know it was there but nobody came to much grief. It was a very happy time there. I would not do it of course but in fact some of the younger lads got involved with the local red- light girls. They were so pally with them that they used to let them put the score on the slate, chuckle. The Old Man used to have to settle the bills I think every week. It was a very happy arrangement and nobody came to any grief.

BULLFIGHT

Every Saturday there used to be a bull fight up at Alicante. The Old Man and I, the Purser and strangely enough, the local police chief who happened to be a very nice fella and his lieutenant made up a party and chartered the old local taxi to take us to Alicante. The police in Torrevieja treated us ok. It was the Customs that were the bug bear. The Police Chief took us the fort miles up a very very B class road. I reckon it was a B B B road. The road we used to travel was absolutely rutted. We used to say that the driver picked out a couple of good ruts, put the car into it, started it off and (chuckle) then promptly went to sleep. The car found its own way into Alicante by following the ruts. I wasn't particularly keen on bull fighting. I do not like the idea of the poor old bull but it was surprising the number of times the bull came off best. It was a very colourful affair. All the Spaniards used to treat it like a football match. The excitement was high. The wine skins used to be passed around. I do not know whether you have ever drunk out of a wine skin. Believe me it is a work of art. When I first tried it out most of it ended up down my shirt front but, as they say, practise makes perfect.

Alicante was then a beautiful city. A very nice place. There was lots to see. There were some very very good restaurants and we always had a good blow out. A very enjoyable day. We used to come back of a night to Torrevieja. No lights anywhere. The taxi had problems with his lights but that did not seem to worry the Spaniards. As I said they used to find a suitable rut. Get into it and stay in it as long as he got to Torrevieja. It was very interesting that kind of living.

SHIP OUT LIKE A BLOODY BULLET

The locals said we would never get off. As I said we were there for six months. I thoroughly enjoyed it. We used to invite the locals on board. We could not entertain them. We just showed them around. They brought their friends from far and wide and they loved it. They never saw a ship so close, without any water around it. We had a lot of surveyors down. A lot of people. Superintendents down from the Office in Cardiff arranging this and arranging that and the other bloody thing. A Swedish and a British salvage crowd got together and made an assessment of what was involved. We were in on the discussions and they said that the only way they could get the ship off was to blast a channel out through three reefs we had come through. That was going to take some time. They would have to wait for similar conditions to arrive to that we went ashore on. The only way they said you would get water there again was when there was a gale blowing or a mistral coming down from the Gulf of Lyons.

This is what transpired. The salvage tugs arrived and got their salvage crews going. We were left with a skeleton crew. All the sailors and ratings were taken off the ship and taken home. There was only myself, the Captain and one other Officer, a bosun and a few engineers. Altogether there were nine of us left aboard the ship and we were there to look after the owner's interests.

When the salvage people took over a ship they more or less have control of the ship. We were there to watch the interests of the owners to see that ship's stores and all this kind of stuff were not pilfered. Generally, to hold a watching brief and to assist where possible. I took a very active part in the salvage operations. I was very interested in it. It is quite an experience and I entertained ideas of going into salvage. The salvage people offered me a job but I did not take it up.

We eventually got off Torrevieja pretty well under the same conditions as we got on. It started to blow one night. By now the reefs were open and they had all the ground gear out, the big heavy tackles, to help to pull off the ship. The tugs were all connected up and the winds started to come up and the sea started to come up, which was the important thing. You could feel her shaking. Then like a bloody bullet out of a gun she started to move. She went out of those reefs there like a speed boat. She nearly ran down one of the tugs that had us in tow but did not. Anyway, they got her off. Got her out to sea and held her out there until the mistral dropped again and that was that. We rode the gale out and when the wind dropped and when the swell went down, we dropped anchor. We were then about three miles off the Port. All is well that ends well.

AMIGO AMIGO FAREWELL

We came off so fast that, of course, we left a lot of stuff ashore, especially the ship's laundry. Lots of official documents had to be collected from the Customs and, of course, we had to get a clearance to sail and lots of other things. The Old Man and I went ashore. He did the business of collecting the documents.

I chartered the one and only taxi that was in Torrevieja and I went to the farmhouse where the woman of the farmhouse used to do our washing. She did not charge us a hell of a lot for it but it was very handy believe me. She used to make a good job of it too. God, she did not know what to say. They thought we were there on the beach for the rest of our lives. She was in tears. She made an awful fuss of me. Put her arms around me "Amigo Amigo" (chuckle). I eventually got the laundry. I got into the taxi and got back down to the ship, met the Old Man and we went into the club to see the members.

They and the whole town were excited. It was the greatest thing that had happened to that town I think ever by the sound of it. Everybody was out. All wishing us farewell. Some of them were even crying. I never saw anything like it. We went into the club. Met a few members there and had a few farewells.

THE BLOODY CUSTOMS

The only problem we had was with the bloody Customs. He was the big noise. He was the power in the town. One of Franco's men. Franco ran the place and, of course, it was a dictatorship. He was the Chief of Customs. He really was the big man. It was trying to get our clearance from him that we ran into problems. We eventually got them and he cleared us to sail but he made all kinds of difficulties for the salvage people. They had to pay this and they had to pay the other thing and, of course, if he did not release the salvage crowd the ship itself was not going to go anywhere. Anyway, they paid him off.

One of the tugs picked us up and took us in tow. We started for Gibraltar. The other salvage tug set about collecting up his salvage gear, like the ground anchors, tackles, and stuff that he had used for the salvage purposes and cleared everything up. As it happens this Custom's fella had a very, very, classy looking yacht in the fishing port. Not very big but it was beautifully appointed and really classy. It was all part of the bribes.

I HEARD THIS TALE AFTERWARDS

The night before the second tug sailed, they were anchored outside the breakwater. They made a secret re-entry into the harbour in their motor launch and went alongside the Customs man's beautiful yacht. They dumped about a gallon of nitric acid underneath the floorboards. I do not think that yacht would have been of much use to him in after years.

HOME

We were proceeding down to Gibraltar. We got there eventually and went into one of the dry docks. They started to make the underwater examination. Lloyds, surveyors and all the rest of it. As I said the skin of the ship had not been pierced at all. The floors were up and the keel was buckled but she was not actually making water into the holds. The double bottoms, of course, were flooded but they went over all the rivets that had been affected, re-riveted. Did a lot of welding. Eventually they made us seaworthy enough to go with a tug escort to Falmouth.

We used our own engines. We steamed from Gibraltar and went up to Falmouth where we laid up while tenders were put out to the various repair firms. This takes a bit of time because they have to come down and make their own inspections and the ship had to be docked in Falmouth so as everybody could inspect her.

Eventually the tenders were put through and a firm in Middlesborough got the contract. We then went around the coast and went to Smith's dock in Middlesborough where we spent the next nine months repairing. The repairers had to pretty well rebuild the under section of the ship and then the engines had to be taken out and relined. The propeller shaft was all out of line. It was a major operation. I think the repair bill was getting on for about half a million pounds, which was quite a sum of money in those days.

That was in 1952 I think. I rather enjoyed it because Babe and our daughter came to stay with me regularly during the nine months. We saw quite a lot of the northeast coast then. We had some good friends up there that used to drive us all over the place. You would not think Middlesbrough was a very beautiful part of the world but it is surprising. You were right into the Yorkshire Dales and it is a really beautiful country. I came home to Liverpool quite often. In fact, I went over to Ireland and saw them there.

HARRY'S GRAY'S DEATH

When I was home on leave, Babe's father Harry Gray died. It was rather tragic the way he did. We were sitting in the kitchen in September Road just chatting after supper. He had been off colour for a few days. He and I were sitting on the settee when he suddenly just keeled over on me. Knocking me sideways with him lying over me. I realised it was serious. He was having a haemorrhage. There was an awful mess all around the place. I got hold of his pulse and felt the life going out of him. I tried to revive him as best I could but I knew it was hopeless. Babe had been next door to dial 999 and the police and ambulance came very quickly. Myself, Babe and May took Harry to the hospital. Poor old Harry was dead before he left his own home. He was certified dead when we arrived at Broadgreen Hospital. It was an awful occasion, especially for his wife and daughters. He was one of the nicest men I had the good fortune to meet and have as a father- in- law. I remember that night I was feeling pretty shook up and called into Charlie Whelan's pub at the top of September Road. "Charlie I will have a double rum." I downed it in no time and said, "Give me another one Charlie." He said, "What the hell is wrong with you. You usually have a pint of bitter." "Well, I have a good reason for it," and told him why. "Christ, I think I will join you in a double rum," which he did. Charlie was only hanging on too. He was another dying craitor as they say. He knew Harry well enough, although he was not a drinking man at all. He seldom went out for a drink. The only time I think he ever did was with me.

MAY GRAY DIED, BURIED IN IRELAND

Mrs Gray never really got back to her old self after that. I think it was about a year later that she died. It happened in Herrylock. She was very fond of Ireland

and very fond of her home district, which, as we know, is Herrylock, Templetown, down by the Hook. She suddenly had this urge that she would like to go for a holiday, even though she was not too well. Babe said, "Well I will take you." I was away again at sea by this time. It was while they were over there in the old homestead that May took ill. She lasted for several days. Babe did all the nursing and looked after her, which she was very glad and pleased to do. The neighbours were the best in the world. They helped no end but May died.

She had expressed a wish that she would like to be buried in Templetown in the old graveyard. There are no undertakers down there. The neighbours do all that is necessary, even to some of the men folk going down and opening up the old family grave. It was just a simple funeral. The coffin was carried by the men from the house to the graveyard.

That was the end of poor May. She was a lovely woman. I keep on saying this but she was one of the nicest women that I ever had the good fortune to be with and be the son in law of. Both her husband and her were well matched. I can only say God be good to the two of them. It is a pity there is not a few more like them around.

As I think I said before we lived with Babe's parents. They were very considerate people, did not live in our pocket and we certainly did not live in theirs, even though we lived in the same house. We came and went and nobody said, "Where are you going?" or "What are you doing?" It was that kind of a life and it was a very successful arrangement. I was sorry when it all came to an end.

HOMER CITY – WANDERING AROUND THE WORLD

I left home after all the trouble with Babe's father dying. I went and joined a ship called the Homer City. The old Skipper of that ship was quite a character. Like myself he suffered from a stammer. He was a very nice fella. Not only did he have a stammer he also had very very poor eyesight. In fact, he really should not have been at sea at all in charge of a ship, but that is beside the point. The great thing about the Homer City was that when I joined she had an Indian crew. That is the first time I ever had an Indian crew and I must say it was a marked improvement to having a white crew. I did not know I was alive.

We set off on the voyage and in the process were wandering about the world. We loaded grain down in Freemantle for Calcutta. When we arrived, we found that there was a lot of industrial strife on in the port. All the stevedores were on strike. There were no ships either loading or discharging. I asked the Agent how long we would be there. "Oh about three months." Ye Gods my heart really failed me then.

CALCUTTA

We arrived there about a couple of weeks just before the monsoon broke. About the worst time you could be in Calcutta. The heat and humidity then is, well, beyond comprehension, especially when you are surrounded by millions of Indians.

THE BORE

We ended up in one of the inner docks in Calcutta, which was something anyway. We did not have to worry about the bore that runs up and down the river Hooley. It is quite an impressive thing. I do not know if you have ever heard of it but at certain times of the year you get this bore which runs up the river. The water level in the river can rise as much as twelve feet in seconds. It is an awful problem for ships that are on the river moorings because you do not just suddenly lift a ship twelve feet and then expect nothing to happen.

Well ships used to break adrift from their moorings. There used to be hell and general chaos, mayhem. The drill was that when the bore was expected you could see it coming up the river. In fact, you could hear it. The engines were on, ready for instant use. The crew stood by fore and aft just before the bore struck your area. You slacked off all your moorings as much as you could. Of course, you went up. The ship went up the dockside and then the bore hit you. You rose and it picked up the slack of the moorings. In theory it was supposed to pull you back alongside again but in actual practice it never happened. But that is a little side issue as regards what life in Calcutta in those days was like.

CALCUTTA TEMPLES

We had three months there and it was pretty rough. You know any fresh stuff you buy there is always suspicious. I suppose you realise that. If you journeyed through India yourself you had to be very careful what you ate. What you got from local chandlers was never much good anyway. Life was not at all pleasant.

I had a good look around Calcutta. Had a look at some of the Temples in the immediate vicinity. From that point of view, it was most interesting. I have never seen such work in all my life that has been put into those Indian Temples. How the hell they ever conceived the idea and how they ever brought it to a conclusion is beyond me. When you think of Temples carved out of solid rock. Mountains hollowed out and a Temple built inside. All the statues. All the wonderful carvings. All part of the living rock. We certainly never produced anything like that in our part of the world and yet we are inclined to look on the Indians as not quite on a par with us marvellous white people.

CALCUTTA AGAIN AND AGAIN

We eventually got shut of our cargo and left again back into Fremantle. Another load of bloody grain and back again to the same place – Calcutta. Fortunately, things had picked up a bit and we were not there quite so long on the second occasion. We got our cargo discharged but that was not the end of it. We left again. Came back down to Freemantle, another cargo of grain, back to the same place. I had seen enough of Calcutta to last me for quite some time because the starvation and as I have said stepping over dead bodies in the main Street in Calcutta.

GERALDTON AUSTRALIA

On that particular voyage we finally ended up at Geraldton of all places. The Captain was very well known there. He used to make his headquarters in a pub. I think they call it the Great Northern. It was Great something anyway. He never lived aboard ship. He used to live at the Hotel attached to the pub. He was a personal friend of the owners. They looked after him very well. It was a typical Australian pub. In those days there was lots of tough looking Aussies there at the bar, downing as much beer as fast as they could.

On that voyage the Captain became ill and either side of that he had enough. In fact, he was relieved at Geraldton. He did not leave the ship. He came home with us as a passenger but that was his final voyage as a ship's Master. They gave him a farewell party at this Great Northern in Geraldton and I have never seen the likes of it before. They really pulled out the stops. You know it was one of the best dos that I had ever been to and, of course, it was a really boozy do. I think half of Geraldton must have been drunk that night but it was a very, very, enjoyable occasion, laugh. Another Skipper took over eventually.

We used to have great parties at Geraldton. The locals were very hospitable. We used to take some time loading in those days. The loading arrangements there twenty odd years ago where to say the least antiquated. It took quite a while to load a full cargo of grain, which gave us time to put in quite a bit of shore leave. We used to have some quite good parties on board too. We used to invite the locals on board to return the hospitality they gave to us. Of course, having the Indian crews you could lay on pretty good barbecues and curry parties and all that kind of stuff.

In the end you know we used to be glad to sail from Geraldton just to get a full night's sleep! Every night was booked when you were away out in the middle of the bloody bush in a farmer's place or some place. It was always a great big boozy party. Drinking beer out of barrels and great barbecues – king prawns, all sorts of shellfish. I was never a great lover of this but I could go a good steak ok. We used to have some great times down there.

A ship arriving in Geraldton in those days was an occasion. It was something of interest to the locals to come down. We always had visitors on the ship. They used to wander around. We did not put any brakes on them. They came from far and wide.

MOST BORING DRIVE

I drove on one occasion for a weekend from Geraldton down to Perth with some of the locals. They were going down there on business and they took me along with them. It was the most boring bloody drive I have ever seen in my life. It seems one long straight Road all the way from Geraldton to Perth. I did not enjoy that part of it very much at all. The scenery is much the same for most of the way anyway and a lot of driving was done at night. They would drive like bloody hell those fellas. Apart from sighting the occasional kangaroo that was the only interest we had. But we had a great time down in Perth. We did all the pubs. A great time was had by one and all. We eventually got back, chuckle, safely. I would not do it again though.

I expect I would not know Geraldton now. I suppose it has all changed but it was nice down there. I went water skiing in the harbour there. That was the first time I ever went water skiing. I did not make a bad effort at it. I soon cottoned on to it and quite enjoyed it. When I think back about it that place down there is full of bloody sharks. They had a swimming pool there in those days that was netted off. There were huge nets all around it and people swam in there. But when we were on the ship, we swam off the side.

CAPTAIN'S AMAZING PARROT

I was Chief Officer. The old Skipper had his wife on board. He had a parrot and the parrot and him were great pals. He was a typical old sea dog with a parrot. The parrot used to literally camp on his shoulder. The only thing the Skipper did not have was a peg leg. Then he would really have looked the part. This ruddy parrot was nearly human. He could do what he liked with the bird. Anybody else the bloody old parrot used to attack them.

Of an evening, he invited the Chief Engineer and me up to his room at about eight o'clock, after I came off watch for a talk. I used to be on the four to eight watch. We were regaled with drinks. He was very generous. As much drink as you wanted as long as you kept him company for an hour.

As soon as we went into his accommodation the bloody parrot used to attack us. He used to go for our ears and we dare not swipe it because the old Skipper would have taken exception. He would not have liked it. So, we had to try and defend ourselves. Trying to retain our ears and keep him at bay, we managed to get our drinks down us.

We were anchored off Bombay, waiting for a berth. All the ships were not in the Port. We were outside at anchor waiting to berth. It was during the southwest monsoon. One warm day the old Skipper decided he would open one of his windows and the parrot took advantage of it and flew out of the window. There was consternation. Because a parrot that is in captivity was unable to fly very far there was a great worry he would end up in the water. He was not used to flying anyway but the wind took him and he couldn't get back. I happened to be on the bridge at the time. I picked up a pair of binoculars and I kept them trained on him. Eventually I saw him land on a Greek ship, which was about a quarter of a mile away.

We launched the life boat and the Chief and myself and one or two of the crew members set off for the Greek ship. It was hard going, with the southwest monsoon in Bombay, in the open anchorages it is not very pleasant, there is quite a sea running.

Anyway, we eventually got over to this Greek ship. I had the parrot's cage in my hand. I got on the companion way, or the ladder as you might call it and walked up the ship's side to the deck. On the deck there were four or five Greek sailors and they were looking at me as I stepped on to the deck with this cage in my hand. They could not speak English and we couldn't speak Greek. After making a few signs and a few sickly leers at them, trying to make myself understood, without any joy, I walked straight up on to the bridge.

I guessed that the old boy would be in the wheel house, where he used to be on our own ship. Lo and behold, I went into the wheelhouse and there was Cocky the parrot. He was perched on the steering wheel, looking awful bloody miserable. He saw me coming with his cage and I am sure his features changed if that is possible with a bird. If ever a parrot had a look of relief on this face, I am sure he had. I opened the cage and without further ado, much to my surprise, he hopped straight into it and I shut the door on him. He offered no resistance. On our own ship you could never get him into the cage. The times we were trying to get him into the cage for the old Skipper to go on the bridge and so that he would not get away whilst on the bridge, we used to put him in the cage and we used to have a hell of a job.

Now I had a cage with a parrot in it. The Greeks looking at me because they did not know the damn parrot was up in their wheelhouse and they wondered what was going on but I did not make any bones about it. I said "Farewell" and down the gangway back on to the boat. We eventually restored Cocky to his rightful owner the Captain. If I had given him the crown jewels he could not have been more pleased, chuckle.

When we eventually got alongside in Bombay his wife decided to leave the ship and go home. The P & O had a run out there. They had three liners called the Three White Sisters. She went home on one of those. The Captain and I were there seeing her off. We eventually discharged our grain, loaded iron ore for Japan and went off down the Malay Straits. We bunkered in Singapore. Finally ended up in Japan, where we discharged our cargo of iron of iron ore.

HIROSHIMA

I should tell you that on that same ship, Homer City, I arrived in Japan with grain. This is when the Japs were really in a poor way. They were still on very short rations from their war time defeat and they received us with open arms. Food in those days in Japan was very, very, scarce. I remember the Mayor of the city coming down with a bunch of flowers to welcome the ship. I had never had any bloody use for them after the way they treated their prisoners of war and I certainly had no sympathy for them. They were very good to us pre-war. Very nice, interesting people. The war changed them. It brought out the evil in them. They were cruel to thousands of people. China had no use whatsoever for the Japanese.

On a previous occasion, within about six months after the atom bomb was dropped on Nagasaki and Hiroshima, I was down there in a ship and saw the ruins of the place. It was horrific to say the least. You know that place must have been radioactive. All kinds of awful contagious stuff lying about but there were no restrictions placed on us. We wandered all over the place. We did not know you could be affected by this fall out and all the rest but it was all there and I am sure if we had Geiger counters they would have blown up. Fortunately, I have had no problems. Maybe it is more my good luck than anything else. When you read what this kind of stuff can do to your health. People, soldiers, that took part in the actual testing of the atom bomb, a lot of those poor fellas died of cancer or leukaemia. I never heard of any of the people I was with having any adverse effects but I suppose it could have happened.

It was an awful thing to see the city of Hiroshima. You would never think it was a city. It was just wreckage. Just absolute level wreckage with the occasional reinforced building still partially standing but very few of them. I often thought then any nation that would use the bomb again in any subsequent war would have to be bloody crazy. No nation could win any war with a weapon like that, especially if the other side had similar weapons. I always had an idea that that bomb would prevent wars, at least major wars anyway. So far so good it has.

NEW WESTMINSTER CITY

I had been on the Homer City quite some time and felt it was time for a change. We took the ship back to the U.K. and I left the ship there. I had several months leave due to me and on the expiry of that they kept me at home so that I could join a new ship they were building in Sunderland. I had three months at home before I joined the New Westminster City at Sunderland and had another two months in Sunderland overseeing the completion of the building. I used to come home every weekend. It was quite a nice arrangement. When the accommodation was finished and everything was lined up my wife and daughter came and stayed with me on the ship. It was a nice time. We went back to Wexford during my leave. I signed on the New Westminster City June 1956 and eventually left her in Hamburg in July 1959. Three years on that ship. That is a good spell. I think that is the longest I ever spent on any ship. My last voyage as Chief Officer. She was a particularly nice ship. The accommodation was superb. I had my own Office. My own day room. My own bedroom and my own bathroom. I could not fault it. We had an Indian crew. The food was excellent. Life was very pleasant. The only difficulty was again being away from home. I was on her, as I said, for three years. One voyage lasted sixteen months without getting back to the U.K. Too long to be away from your family as far as I was concerned but I did have family with me on coastal voyages.

During my time on that ship, we came into Limerick and discharged grain there. I had all the crowd down from Thurles. All the Dwans came down. My sister Maureen's daughter Mary married

Frank Dwan. They had a very nice time with several meals on board and were very impressed with the ship.

In later years I joined her as Master. We followed the usual trading patterns. Grain from the U.S.A. to Japan and grain from the west coast of Australia and back to the U.K. or the Continent. We had several time charters in between too. Mostly by U.S. firms, which were always interesting.

INDIAN FISHERMEN IN DIRE STRAITS

On the first trip we loaded general cargo at several ports in India and were on our way to Rangoon to pick up some jute. We came across fishermen who had been blown offshore and were in dire straits. No water, no food. They were on their last legs. There was about twenty of them on board. All they wanted was to get off that fishing boat as soon as they could. We offered to revictual them and give them water and the right directions where to proceed but they would not have it. They just came aboard us and said, "Do what you like with the fishing boat." In the end, we left. We had set it on fire because it would have been a danger to ships in the vicinity if there had been any ships in that part of the world. It was rather a lonely part but then again some fella could have come along and bumped into it.
We took them into Rangoon and landed them there. I think there was about twenty of them. The buggers had the cheek to try and claim the value of the fishing boat and catch the ship's owners. Our Indian crew who could speak the lingo told the authorities that they abandoned the boat of their own free will.

We discharged our general cargo in West Indies. Loaded grain at Corpus Christi and took it to

Japan. Home via Geraldton which was my second home those days. Every time we went there we had parties and carrying on. It was life in the fast lane.

CORNISH CITY FIRST COMMAND

It was an old war time ship. A steam ship with a white crew. A drunken bunch to say the least. It was my first permanent command. We sailed out of Birkenhead bound for Morocco to load phosphate for Shanghai communist China.

When I joined the Cornish City my first sight of her was of several drunken sailors trying to negotiate the gangway. My heart sank to say the least but to be honest they turned out not bad fellows at all. Hard workers at sea but drunken bums in port. The logbook was full of fines and all kinds of incidents.

SABOTAGE

We sailed from Birkenhead and dropped the Pilot. We headed for the Irish sea, rounded Anglesey and broke down. The Chief Engineer, his first job as such, reported to me that he had lost the lube oil to his main bearings and would be about twelve hours before repairs could be effected. Nothing for it but try and anchor in the middle of the Irish sea, which we eventually did. I was still within sight of the South Stack lighthouse so I could keep a check on my position. Southwest gales to storm force were imminent. A nice introduction to command experience to say the least. The Chief, poor fellow, after working flat out, finally got the engines back in position again and we got on the way. He came up on the bridge and said, "You'll never believe this but that break down was due to sabotage."

Some of the crowd at the dry dock wished the ship had been doing some repairs before she sailed. The engine room gang apparently had stuffed waste down through the lube oil lines. It was deliberate sabotage. We reported it back by radio and the police were called in. I never did hear what the outcome was. I was not too interested anyway. He was a new Chief and I was a new Master. It was a bit of a tough experience just as you sailed.

We got under way again and eventually sailed down the Irish sea, through the Bay of Biscay and arrived at our port of Morocco, where we loaded phosphate for Shanghai. We were not a very fast ship. We toddled off down through the South Atlantic and bunkered at Cape Town. Then we proceeded leisurely across the South Indian Ocean, came up into the Malay Straits. Eventually into the South China Sea and finally arrived at Shanghai.

SHANGHAI

We had been warned that the Approaches to Shanghai was a restricted area so I applied to the Chinese authorities long before I arrived at the Approaches and asked them to give me a route into the Pilot Station. They acknowledged my cable but did not give me any routes so I went into the Pilot Station as per the sailing directions, which were the only way I knew of. I eventually got in there and picked up the Pilot. Twenty armed Marines came aboard at the same time. I did not like the look of them buggers.

ALL KINDS OF COMMISSARS

Eventually we tied up in the Wang Po River at Shanghai. I was boarded by all kinds of Commissars, all demanding to know why I had sailed through a restricted area and accusing me of being a capitalistic spy. There must have been about ten of them in my room, all gabbing away in Chinese. They had one so called interpreter. My interrogation lasted about four hours. My only defence being that I had applied for a route into the Pilot Station from the Port Authorities but none had been forthcoming. I showed them my cable and I showed them their acknowledgement. Believe me I was getting worried.

The Chinese Reds at that time were a very stroppy bunch and hated us foreign devils. In the end I had to type a letter of apology to the authorities. My approach charts were confiscated and all shore leave denied us. Anyway, that did not concern me. We were alongside and I had not been slung in jail and they started to discharge the ship. I was appalled at the way they were discharging. Phosphate is a very very dusty cargo and if there is any wind at all it just blows away. They were discharging the stuff on to the quay just in canvas slings. They just dumped it on the quay. I do not know whether you have been to Shanghai but there is always wind blowing in that part of the world. It was just like a fog blowing all this bloody cargo away. There were fellas coming down with those bicycle rickshaws with a kind of a little tub on the back of it and they were shovelling this phosphate into it and dragging it away. There did not seem to be any mechanised transport at all. The most bloody inefficient way of discharging a ship I ever saw. All over the quay they had loudspeakers fixed, all babbling away in Chinese. We afterwards learned from some of the Agents that this was exhorting the workers to work hard and save this cargo and it was all for the People's Republic. Comparing different gangs and the gang had done so many others have done hundreds of tons more than other gangs. This was how they were working. They were so bloody childish. Half of our bloody cargo must have gone into the Wang Po River if I was any judge of it. Anyway, in the end the authorities relented and they allowed us shore leave. We were there for weeks the way they were discharging that cargo was painful.

NOTHING MUCH TO SEE OR DO

I wandered ashore a few times but there was nothing much to see. It certainly was not the Shanghai that I had known in my younger days. Shanghai used to be a wide-open part of the world believe me. The sky was the limit there but under the Chinese Reds it was like a bloody big graveyard. It was full of people all running backwards and forwards but they didn't seem to be doing anything. There was nothing in the shops. There was nothing you could buy. There was no amusement. There were no pubs. There was nothing you know where you could have a drink.

THE INTERNATIONAL CLUB

They had an International Club which all Communist States used to have in their various ports. It was called the Bangers Club. It was a fabulous place inside, or what was left of it after the ravages of being taken over by the communists. You could see it had been a fabulous place. There was teak all over the place and beautiful carvings and all the rest of it. Now it was turned over to a bunch of dirty sea man from all over the world. They were supposed to be selling beer in there but nobody could drink it. There was nothing in there. There was nothing to buy. You could not even buy the normal Chinese stuff like jade. Some of the Chinese pottery was very beautiful but there was none of it available at all.

SHANGHAI SPY CONSCIOUS

Life there was very boring. There were guards all over the place. They were checking your pass here and they were checking your pass there and they did not know whether your pass was the right side up. They just looked at it and made gestures with their side arms and it was not very pleasant at all. You felt as if anything could happen. They were all very spy conscious. Everybody on British ships or foreign ships were all classified as spies. Anybody that owned a camera was really suspect. All cameras and anything like that had to be put in bond before you arrive there so nobody did have any cameras.

I was glad when I eventually got the ship finished and made preparations to sail again. I explained to them the only way I knew of getting out of China was through the Admiralty sailing directions. I showed them on the chart. I asked them, "Will you give me a route out so that there will be no problems?" You will not believe this. They said, "Oh no Captain you follow the route you came in on." After bloody putting me through four hours of bloody interrogation they told me to go out the same way as I came in. What the hell was restricted I do not know. We eventually got to sail from Shanghai.

BASRA

After leaving Shanghai we went down to Brisbane, Australia and loaded grain for Basra. We took that up, going inside the Barrier Reef, out across the Islands, around the South China Sea and finally finding our way up into the Malay Straits and across the Indian Ocean into the Arabian Gulf and on into the Persian Gulf. Finally arriving at Basra. We tied up in Basra. The heat during the day was, at times, 130 degrees Fahrenheit. The heat inside that old ship, she had steam pipes running along the bloody accommodation, must have been well over 130 degrees Fahrenheit. How the bloody hell we survived that lot I just do not know but there you are.

We were tough in those days, chuckle. We were there for several weeks. It was a bloody awful time. It was ok ashore. The Agents were pretty good to me and to the rest of us. They used to take us ashore. We were made members of the British Residents Club, which was rather a luxurious place. You would get a decent glass of beer there. There was a swimming pool that you could use but aboard the ship itself was most unpleasant for everybody. I had a lot of people ill with all kinds of heat problems. You know, dehydration all that kind of stuff. I was glad to get going again.

We went back down to Australia. This time to Bunbury. We loaded grain, again this for the U.K. We took that cargo back to Belfast, of all places, to discharge there. I did not leave the ship. The family came over to me. They had a little over a week with me, which was not too long after a long voyage.

We signed off the old crew and signed on a fresh crew. The new crew were all fellas from Belfast.

They were bloody hard nuts but I found them, in the course of the voyage, to be good sailor men. Good men at their job. They worked hard at sea. We had no problems with them except for the fact that when they got into port, they used to go haywire, drinking and fighting and all that kind of stuff. They just ended up in bloody jail. But, as I said, there was not much harm in them. I have sailed with a lot worse in my earlier days.

We signed on at Belfast and went across to New Orleans and loaded another cargo of grain, this time for Yokohama. New Orleans was another part of the world which, at certain times of the year, is very, very oppressive. The heat and humidity there is unbearable but, of course, New Orleans is quite a place to go ashore in. There is plenty to see and plenty to do. So that was not too bad. We eventually sailed out of New Orleans, went through the Panama Canal, and wended our way across Yokohama, where we discharged our cargo of grain.

GOA CREW ENDED UP IN JAIL

On completion of discharging in Japan we had to go to Goa, Margoa they call it, to load iron ore. We eventually arrived at Margoa. You do all your loading there while at anchor. There are no docks or piers and the iron ore comes out in local craft. It is a very, very, long winded slow business. It took us three weeks to load our cargo. I had a lot of problems with the crew. In those days Margoa was under the Portuguese authorities. Drink was as cheap as water is in some places. You name it, you could get all the finest brands of whiskies and all the liquors and all the beers at cost price. That was without any excise duties whatsoever on it. Our crew was on the shore overnight and they were making whoopie. They were drinking Drambuie out of half pint glasses. In the end every bloody one of them ended up in jail. They wrecked several bars and created all kinds of mayhem.

They even fought with the Portuguese police. I was without a crew. I had one or two fellas and apprentices to run the ship. The rest were all in jail. I had to go ashore and see what I could do about this. I got hold of my Agent and we went up to the local police to ask what the prospects were. They said there were no prospects. They were not allowing them fellows out for at least forty-eight hours. The ship was not sailing. We were still loading cargo so we did not really need them. They said they would all be fined heavily and they would have to pay for all the damage that occurred. I said, "Could I see those fellows? Could I go into the jail and see them?" I was allowed to go in. I have never seen such a bloody horrible place in all my life. Talk about the Black Hole of Calcutta. It was really a stinking hole. I was talking to some of them that were capable of talk. They had been beaten up. I mean probably all of it was while they were fighting the police while outside but they had really lain into them with their truncheons. They had beaten some of them very badly. There was nothing I could do for them. They said they were not even given water to drink. I had to go and beg the warders, "Give those fellows water." Whilst I was there, they at least got water. They were not too interested in food.

In the heel of the hunt some of them were there for over three days. I had to pay all the damages, which amounted to quite a bit. Of course, it all came out of their wages eventually. They were all put aboard the ship and there was no more shore leave. They were not allowed to put their foot in

Margoa again while the ship was in port. I did not object to that. At least the buggers were quiet.

INDIAN SURGEON OPERATING WHILST SMOKING

We were there for three weeks. Apart from this kind of an incident it was quite interesting. I went around with the Agent quite a bit. Myself and the Chief Engineer drove around through the various parts. It is a very historical place. There is a great shrine there to St. Francis Xavier. Part of his body is preserved in the Cathedral. It is very interesting to go in and see it. There were some very good restaurants. We had some very good meals.

One of my catering staff, a young fella, had a fall on the ship and he had what they called a double hernia. He needed to be operated on. I had him landed and taken to the local hospital. They said they would do the operation. I said, "OK that's fine." The following day I went to see how he was getting on and said, "Can I see the Surgeon that did the operation?" They said, "He is in the operating theatre at the moment." "Oh, I will wait until he comes out." They said, "Oh no, no, no. You can go in there and see him." "I'm not sterile and all the rest of it." They said, "It does not matter. You are in India now." They were Portuguese but they could speak pretty good English so I went in there.

You will not believe this. There was some fellow on the table. It was not my fellow but another fellow. They were doing something. There was this Surgeon in there and one nurse. What they were doing I did not look too closely but I noticed on a side table there was a cigarette in an ash tray and it was lit. That Surgeon was working on this fellow and while I was there, he went over and he had a puff on his cigarette, put it down again and came back over and carried on with what he was doing with this fellow on the table.

When he eventually got out and I was talking to him I said, "I am flipping horrified. Don't you have any idea of hygiene here?" He said, "You are not in Europe now. You could not kill those fellows out here with the kind of bugs that would see you and I off. They are immune to all kinds of viruses. It doesn't make any impression on them. They have lived with viruses and diseases all their life. When they come into a place like this, I have not got to take those precautions. I mean that." I said, "Ye Gods. How is my fellow getting on?" He said, "We gave him special treatment. We washed our hands before we operated on him."

Well, the guy that had that operation survived ok. He did not come back to the ship. He was not fit for duties so I eventually had him flown home. Believe me, when I saw the inside of that hospital, boy I was horrified. But, you know, that is how things are. Things go on. People here back in the U.K. and I suppose people in Australia, just cannot credit that this is the kind of condition that exists in various parts of the world.

You know in India they do operations on the eyes out in the open street, with flies all over the place. They take cataracts from people's eyes. The Surgeon said, "If we do not do it like this they will never get done. They will be blind all their lives. What we are doing now I agree the conditions are not all that good but they have a chance. Those people can put up with an awful lot of infection without coming to any harm."

CREW MAN APPENDICITIS

Another time I treated one of the crew for appendicitis on advice from the Liner and eventually got him into the Port of Chicago. I was in touch with a Liner giving strict instructions to get to a designated Port as soon as possible. The Liner was a long distance away from me otherwise he said he would have done it you know. He said, "You will be in Port before we can contact you." Contacting people at sea upsets their routine. They do not like intervention at sea in case they do the wrong thing. They could be in trouble.

In the Master's medicine chest, they think of everything you know. I once sewed a man's injury up.

BURIAL AT SEA

He was buried according to International Law. For the Service we all dressed in uniform. I read the International Burial Service. The ship would be just about stopped.

We sewed him up in canvas and put in heavy weights so he would sink before launching him over the side. The end of the hatch board would be on the ship's side. The other end would be on a drum. I buried one fella and the water was so clear. It was not very deep. It was only about twenty fathoms. We could see his body going down to the bottom and we could see him there. We could see big fish and everything. I thought it was a lovely way to be buried.

Once again, we got our cargo of iron ore on board and went back to Japan. We discharged into a place called Chiba. No problems there. We eventually sailed and made our way down to

Freemantle. Another cargo of grain. This time we took it back to Leith in Scotland and discharged it there. I left the ship then and reckoned I was due leave. Anyway, I had had enough of white crews. I was looking forward to getting on to an Indian crewed ship again. I had got used to the Indian way of life. I liked the food. I liked the service too. So, I was not too sad to leave the Cornish City.

LEEDS CITY INDIAN CREW

I was not ashore too long though until I had to do a relief job on a ship called the Leeds City. She was also an Indian crewed ship. I was not on her very long. I had to take her from Birkenhead around to Belfast, again with part cargo for Limerick. I took the two girls with me. They came around the coast. We eventually paid off at Belfast and we all came home from there.

KING CITY

I had several months at home then before I had to join my next ship the King City. A very nice- looking ship. She had an Indian crew too. The only problem with that ship was she was inclined to be a bit unstable. You had to be very careful when you were loading light cargoes. She was ok with iron ore and stuff like that but when it was something that filled your upper spaces, even with grain cargo, you had to be very careful. She was very, very, tender. She was not a very nice ship to be on. I had to stick her for a year and a half before I could honestly leave her. I think my first trip we sailed from Sunderland and went down to Torrevieja in Spain. That is where I had all the fun and games in the old Paris City some years ago. When I arrived in Torrevieja and they recognised me as being the Mate of the Paris City I was damn near given the freedom of the port. They gave me a wonderful time. I was number one and I had a grand time. The people were very, very, friendly. They did not know what the hell to do with me. I really enjoyed it. We set sail out of Torrevieja and made our way across the Mediterranean over to the Suez Canal and down the Red Sea and into the Indian Ocean. Eventually we landed in Japan again. We discharged our cargo at Osaka and no problems. Everything went according to plan.

AMERICA SENT FREE GRAIN TO INDIA

After leaving Japan we had a long ballast passage all the way across to the State, to Longview, where we loaded a full cargo of grain. This time it was destined for Calcutta. It was one of the free gifts of grain that the American were giving the Indians at the time. We hauled that down through the Panama Canal and right down south into the South Atlantic and bunkered at Durban this time. We carried on across the Indian Ocean.

IN YOUR STRIDE

On the way in, just before we got to Calcutta, one of the Indian sailors had a heart attack. We had to work on him. We had to give him an injection of morphine to kill the pain. Anyway, the poor bugger was alive when we eventually arrived and he was hospitalised in Calcutta. I never heard what happened to him but he was certainly alive when he left us. That is some of the little problems you have when you are a Master of a ship but you took it all in your stride.

CALCUTTA AN AWFUL EXISTENCE

We were in Calcutta during the hot spell again and Calcutta was always, always, a depressing place to be. I do not know if you have ever read that book, I think they call it Sin City. If you have not, read it, it is worth reading. What they say about the poor in Calcutta is quite true. It is not living. It is an existence and a very, very, grim existence at that. You know, when you look at certain parts of Calcutta you see how affluent it used to be under the White Raj and even to this day under the Indians. Some of the Indians live very well, while the majority of them are in dire straits.

I always left that part of the world with a guilty conscience when, you know, you saw people scavenging in your waste bins. We used to have waste bins at the bottom of the gangway, where you were supposed to dump all your galley refuse and that kind of stuff. You saw people scavenging in that trying to get food. In the end I used to have all this galley refuse parcelled up and wrapped it up properly and not put it in the bin. Just give it to the people. Let them have it. But, as I said, it always depressed me. It is a lovely country but the vast majority of Indians have an awful existence. The people died in the streets wrapped in dirty old rags around them. You can bet your bottom dollar they would never move again. They would be left there for days. The educated do nothing for their people. They should be feeding their people.

HURRICANE

We did not like hurricanes at sea. Trying to manage a ship in those conditions. Many a ship sank. The sea created by a hurricane is all over your head. You can hear the wind coming at you one hundred miles an hour. We used to get conditions sent out from the Weather Office and they would pinpoint the centre of it. We would take steps to avoid it. We would travel on a certain course. We would do our very best to keep out of that curve. Sometimes the thing would stop and back track – not nice.

We were stuck in it for a couple of days. Seas cannoning down on the deck. Hitting the bridge. You cannot do anything. All the deck boards would be screwed down. You cannot go on deck. It was difficult in the galley to cook food. At times I could not get to the galley. Birds got caught in the middle of it and they could not get out of it. Flying around the centre, which strangely enough was quite calm. The centre of any storm is. The birds would be going round and round and in the end you had thousands of them landing on the ship. There was not much you could do for them. Any food we had we fed them but they were too scared to eat the food. They were exhausted. In the end they were swept off by the hurricane. They were lost. It was a circular motion. We could not get out of it. We used to try and get into the southern circle which is not as bad as the northern. You have to know what you are doing. Hurricanes in one part of the world. Typhoons in other parts of the world. They were both as bad as one another.

CAPE OF GOOD HOPE WHIRLPOOL FEARSOME EXPERIENCE

We went down to Australia again and loaded another cargo of grain for the U.K. Of course, it is a good long haul from Australia back to London. We did not go to the Suez Canal. We used to come around the Cape. They reckoned the economics of it was better than sending a ship through the shorter distance through the Suez Canal. It used to be quite a pleasant run that.

Sometimes, not always, but sometimes you could get pretty bad weather rounding the Cape of Good Hope. On one occasion I had a very severe experience. They have an unusual sea there. They refer to it as a hole in the sea and it, literally, is similar to that. The ship seems to drive into a massive whirlpool and you are engulfed.

One of Reardon Smith's ships was making more or less the same passage as I was making. It was coming across from Australia, making the coastline opposite South Africa, when it ran into this abnormal sea, which can be quite devastating. It got into very serious trouble. It hit the sea. I was talking to the Skipper afterwards and he said, "It just came out of the blue. I was never so bloody scared in all my life before. One minute it was quite a reasonable day. There was a bit of a swell, a fresh wind blowing. The next minute I was looking up at the bloody sky and a mountain of seas coming on top of me. It was really a fearsome experience."

The sea damn near flattened everything he had on his fore deck. It took away his mast house and it took the mast along with it. It stove in his number one hatch. It wrecked everything, anything that was movable, ships rails, the lot. Everything went over the side or was wrapped around winches and things.

The Mate, who happened to be in the wheelhouse at the time said the sea came along and smashed in the wheelhouse windows and knocked out the steering gear. In smashing the windows, the poor old Mate, unfortunately, got a shard of glass into his right eye and he was in a bad serious condition.

After they finally managed to get themselves out of this disaster, the Skipper had to make a decision, try and go into East London, which wasn't too far away. It is a very small port. There are no facilities there. You can load and discharge but there are no facilities for repairs. He realised if he went in there, he would not get out again. They would not give him a clearance, due to the ship being unseaworthy. So, he telegraphed in to say that he had a seriously injured man and would the pilot boat meet them inside the break waters and he would land the injured man to have him hospitalised immediately. He said he would not anchor. He would turn the ship around in between the break waters and carry on. He realised if he stopped in East London he would have been there for months.

The poor old Mate was safely landed. He lost the sight of his eye, of course, but subsequently recovered. He never went to sea gain. He was awarded very substantial damages and he got himself a nice little job ashore. It was very unfortunate but he came out as well as could be expected.

The ship in question staggered into Cape Town about a day and a half later. They had the facilities in Cape Town to really go to town and they carried out temporary repairs. They sealed up all the openings that had been opened by the sea. Fixed its hatches and gave it a seaworthy certificate and was able to continue with the voyage. The ship reached the U.K., discharged its cargo and, of course, dry docked. We subsequently carried on with our voyage and got around the Cape without any problems. We arrived in London and my good lady wife and daughter came down while we were discharging the cargo. We had about fourteen days together. We discharged the cargo and went into dry dock afterwards. All too soon the old story of seeing them off at the railway station. The painful goodbyes and we were off again for another world cruise. We went across to Montreal in ballast where we were time chartered by an American Firm to load general cargo, eventually for Japan, calling at Mexico on route to top up with general cargo. At Montreal they had just opened the new Weiland Ship Canal and seaway and oceangoing ships were now able to penetrate to the Great Lakes.

I had the honour of being the first ship in our Firm to find their way into that particular part of the world. We subsequently loaded at Chicago and Detroit and I must say it was a very interesting experience. I think we were about five or six hundred feet above sea level when we were loading in Chicago. I had a good look at Chicago. It was a quite fabulous city. I had a look at the old haunts where Al Capone did all his devilment, chuckle, and you know it was quite interesting. They call it the windy city but there was not too much wind when we were there.

MUSLIM SEAMAN'S BURIAL CHICAGO

The night before we got into Chicago one of our Muslim seamen died. He was found dead in bed. I did not have a chance to bury him at sea. I had to retain the body and report it to the Authorities at Chicago when I arrived there, which I did.

Now there was a bit of a problem because a Muslim has to have special burial rites and as it was a Muslim crew I was more or less bound to see that he got this. I got hold of the Agent and he took me up to an Undertaker. You know a mafia style undertaker, chuckle. You never saw anything like the place. It was like a five-star Hotel. Luxury all over the place and all this horrible soft music playing.

I saw the Undertaker, a very suave-looking gentleman and explained what was involved. He was nonplussed. This was beyond his experience. He had no experience of burying Muslims or knew anything about it but said he would see what he could do. Possibly was a Muslim community in Chicago where he might be able to get hold of a Mullah to do the funeral. He wanted to know what I wanted for the funeral. The first thing was to come in and have a look at the caskets. Well, I went in there and boy I tell you one thing when I kick the bucket, I will never have a casket like the ones he was showing me. There was one of solid mahogany, one of solid brass. You name it they had it. He started off with this casket $5,000. He gradually got down. I eventually settled for an aluminium casket which was $1,000. Right, I said that one. He said, "Oh that." I said, "This poor fellow out in India would be wrapped in a sheet and chucked into a hole. There would be no boxes or anything like that. I much prefer to be able to send this money that I have to pay out for this fancy funeral to this man's relatives back in India. They could well do with the money."

Ok, I had to settle for a hearse and three limousines to take the entourage to the funeral. I think it was the following day. Meanwhile, this Undertaker found a Mullah. That is a Muslim Priest. He had to get all my Muslim crew ashore. They had to attend at the special Chapel of Rest where this fellow was laid out. They had taken his body off the ship and when I saw him again, I did not recognise him. He had a great long grey beard and this had been trimmed and his hair was waved. He was dressed up in a fancy blue suit. He never wore a suit in his life. He looked like a million dollars believe me.

The crew when they came in and saw their ship mate lying there did not recognise him. Anyway, the Mullah was there and the crew were there so I left them to it. It was a Muslim ceremony. After they had finished, he was taken away. The funeral started and we went out to this cemetery. Bodies in the U.S.A. are not allowed to go into the ground. They have got to go into the coffin. The casket has to be put into an airtight and watertight reinforced concrete box which is already in the hole. The only thing they have to do when they put the casket in is to drop the lid on it, which locks itself.

You know that funeral the final bill for that was well over $10,000. I did not mind paying it. I was not paying it so it did not worry me but I just thought if that man had been buried at sea and half of that money had been sent to his wife in India, she could have lived the remainder of her days in comparative comfort. The family were presented with a leatherbound booklet. Very nicely done. A beautiful piece of work. It was sent to his wife in Bombay. No doubt she will still have it if she is alive.

NEW WESTMINSTER CITY

My next ship as Skipper was the New Westminster City. I was quite pleased to get back on that ship. She was a ship that I was particularly fond of when I was Chief Officer on her. She was a very comfortable and extremely good bad weather ship. She had no vices, was easy to handle and maintain. She was well equipped as regards navigational ger. Two radars, telex, latest gyros and radio telephony – short wave radio and local VHF. When I thought of my first command, the old Cornish City, no radar only magnetic compasses. A very antiquated echo sounder and war time radio equipment I was quite proud of myself navigating that old bucket all around the world.

THE WEXFORD SCHOONER

Another little incident during the time I was on the Westminster.

I was in the Seychelles on one occasion on the Westminster, discharging a little bit of cargo from the anchorage. There was no port. I was on the bridge looking at a schooner with my binoculars and thought she was familiar. I had a good look at her and lo and behold she turned out to be the Wexford schooner the Dialinda. She used to be owned by a fellow in Wexford called Captain Cardiff. He was quite a character was Captain Cardiff. He had several daughters. I think my sister Maureen was quite pally with some of them.

It was strange to see this Schooner. She was a lovely Schooner. She had beautiful lines to her. She looked like a yacht actually. Cardiff had sold her years ago and nobody knew where she had got to. She carried cargo backwards and forwards between the Seychelles and Mauritius and also carried passengers. When I say passengers, they were emigrant passengers going from the Seychelles to Mauritius to get seasonal work. I think they used to go down there to pick tea during the season and then they used to come back to the Seychelles. She had a small auxiliary engine when she was in Wexford but on her trading in and around the Seychelles and Mauritius she did all her passages under sail. She never used the auxiliary engine.

I gleaned all this information when I went aboard and had a look at her and spoke to the Skipper. I think he was an Indian but he spoke very broken English. He was very interested in finding out about her when I told him I knew the ship originally – where she had come from.

I wrote to the People newspaper in Wexford saying I had seen the ship. My sister Maureen told me they published the letter. I believe there were a lot of people in the town very interested to hear about this ship. She looked very well then. She was well looked after but where she is now I wouldn't like to say.

My last voyage on the Westminster lasted over twelve months and that was much too long to be away from home. They eventually relieved me and the Chief Engineer in Portland, Oregon. The Chief Engineer had a bit of a nervous breakdown and I 'phoned the Company and told them all about this. The decided the best thing to do was to bring him home and decided to take me off at the same time. I probably should have told you that we had had a relief of Officers during the voyage and the Chief and I were the only people that were left from the original crew that signed on. We were due a relief but apparently when they took the Officers off there was no relief left for me or the Chief. There was nobody available. That was their story anyway and they were sticking to it.

To get home from Portland it meant flying and I had not flown before. I was not too bloody happy with it either. I would have much preferred to have brought the ship home. Anyway, before we went up to the airport my Agent in Portland took me and the Chief out to dinner. We had a damn good meal. We had plenty of hard stuff to go along with it. I was trying to get my nerve up. Anyway, we boarded the plane. It was just a local plane. Apparently, we had to fly from Portland up to Seattle and catch the TWA for Kennedy. I remember the Chief and I taking off from Seattle. Well, the Chief had flown before and he wasn't too bad but I was bloody well petrified in my seat as the plane was revving up to take off. Anyway, we survived it and by the time I got to Kennedy Airport I was quite a hardened flyer and I knew all the answers of course. We had to change planes again at Kennedy Airport for the flight across to Heathrow. It was quite pleasant. I never did really enjoy flying but I had to do quite a lot of flying before I retired. It was policy that the longest they could keep us out was four months. It did not suit to bring the ships home. They used to relieve us all over the world. I had been relieved in Japan and India and even in Hong Kong. I did not object to that. It meant getting home but, as I said, I didn't like flying and I swore that after I retired I would never fly again and I have not.

FIRST CAR

As I said, I flew home from the New Westminster City and had a very good leave. That was when I bought my first car. We had a grand time in that running around the country enjoying ourselves. It was a Vauxhall and I enjoyed that car more than any other subsequent car but that is quite normal. It was around that time we bought a little cottage in North Wales, which was ideal for us. It gave us a lot of interest you know getting the place habitable. It was really a very good pastime. We thoroughly enjoyed our times there. We had that place for over twenty years.

SEXTANT

In tramp ships no part of the world was strange to us. The sextant, otherwise known in the trade as the hambone, due to the shape no doubt, was the only way of ascertaining your position on ocean passages. It was always a surprise to me how accurate the instrument was, together with the chronometer for GMT. If the heavenly bodies were visible you could always get an excellent position. Sights were taken from the wing of the bridge, maybe with very adverse conditions, spraying heavily, rolling, hazy and an ill-defined horizon.

Any part of the world you always put your position down I am here and set your course from there to the next point and in the end say I am here so I must have reached them! When you hit the Indian Ocean and are in the middle of the ocean, then you had to find your way by stars or sun.

The stars were always the best for position. The sun was ok. The planets and the moon were not so good due to the relatively closeness to us. Making a land fall from your latest astronomy sights and coming spot on always gave a lot of job satisfaction. You can never afford to make one mistake when you were navigating. I never got lost. It's nice to be able to say you can find your way all around the world.

Ray McNulty tells me that the sextant is now very rarely used, as all oceangoing ships have satellite navigation. Decca navigators. You get your position at the touch of a button from the characterless computer.

I was pretty good at my job. I got an M.B.E. Been all over the world loading and delivering cargo. A good life. It was certainly interesting from that point of view. As Captain I had a lot of responsibility. I accepted that. That was what you studied for and that was what you were trained for and that was what you eventually became. We had to pass some very stringent exams. Certain types were good Captains. Some not so good. You had to be tuned in to what you were doing.

You can radio on ahead to the Port you are going on to and tell them the day and pretty well the hour you will arrive at it. Sometimes you had to wait for a Pilot. He would come out to you and take you in. We could do it ourselves but it was against the law. You had to have a professional Pilot.

A lot of the ships' Masters retired as Pilots. I had visions of doing that but I said to hell with it. Once you finish with the sea do it completely.

COLUMBUS MUST HAVE HAD ONE

When I started studying for my Second Mate's Certificate, sometime around 1940, I bought a very second-hand sextant from a marine junk shop in Paradise Street in Liverpool. I just got it to practise with. Many a sight I took over the Mersey. When I first took it into the College and showed it to the Lecturer he laughed and said, "Christopher Columbus must have had one very similar to it."

It was an old British Admiralty sextant made by a London firm. They had apparently been out of business since about the turn of the century. So that will give you some idea of the age of it.

As far as I was able to ascertain the sextant had been owned by a Naval Officer and was used when the British Navy was powered by sail only. Its age now must be getting on for 150 to 175 years at least. I still have the receipt for the amount I paid for it two pounds ten shillings. That was in old money. After getting my Second Mate's Certificate I took my old sextant to the Marine instrument makers in Liverpool and had them clean it up and test it for me. Test it for accuracy. To my surprise it had a very small index error, which was noted on the Certificate and was quite satisfactory.

I did not have the money to buy myself a modern sextant so I had to use my old sail boat one. When I first produced it on the bridge to take noon day sights I was the butt of the other Officers and the Old Man when they viewed my prehistoric hambone. Remarks like, "We will probably find ourselves in the middle of the Sahara Dessert," and such like. I agree my attempts at sightseeing on a rolling ship where not up to much and my position was nowhere like the more experienced navigators but as the voyage progressed and I got more proficient at using the hambone my positions came reasonably close to the other Mates.

I used that old hambone all through my professional career. If you can call an instrument, an inanimate object, a friend, well that was and is. It never let me down. We found our way out of many a dicey situation, especially in the islands and reefs of the South China seas and the Malay Straights, the Grand Banks, etc. I have great affection for it and now and then I bring him down for a clean up to turn the vernier and read the scale, although my eyesight is not what it used to be and it is difficult for me now to read my old friend. People tell me my hambone is now quite valuable. I will never part with him. Not a bad price to pay for an instrument that saw me safely about the ocean for well over forty years. I had it serviced only once in all the time I used it at sea. You'll be saying that fella and his old hambone.

RADIO FOUR SATURDAY LIVE PROGRAMME ON SEXTANT 19TH JANUARY 2013

INTRODUCTION

Retired naval Commodore Mark Higgins, now in his nineties, went to sea as a teenager with the Shipping Company Sir William Reardon Smith, sailing tramp ships out of Cardiff to practically everywhere.

In 1940 to get his Officer's Certificate he bought a sextant, that bit of kit made from brass, which navigators look through to establish the angle of the sun or a star from the horizon in order to work out where they are. Mark's was already over one hundred years old when he bought it. It accompanied him through the second World War, on North Atlantic Convoys, the landings in North Africa and in Italy, where his ship delivered mules to carry ammunition up Monte Casino and to bring injured soldiers down again. Mules too can be casualties of war and Mark's ship carried them to a special recuperation Island in the Mediterranean.

After the war he served in the Merchant Marine until his retirement in the late sixties and today he is the oldest living Captain in Reardon Smith and the sextant is the thing about him.

MARK

When I first went to sea was in November 1934, I went to sea in desperation because I come from Southern Ireland, a little town called Wexford and there was absolutely no prospects of any job of any decency there whatsoever, so I decided to go to sea. I applied to the Firm for a cadetship and I have to tell you I was paid the wonderful sum of sixty pounds for the whole four years. My memories were pretty grim. It was hard work. Most of it was spent shovelling coal into bunkers and any other dirty work that could be found on board the ship it was usually the cadets that were saddled with it but at the end of four years there wasn't much about a ship that I didn't know about. You mention any country you like and I have more than likely been there.

The sextant has been in my possession now for seventy years. I would say it is approximately one hundred and fifty to two hundred years old. My fellow Officers on the ships I sailed on they used to refer to my sextant as something that Nelson would have used at the battle of Trafalgar.

It is a handmade instrument. Beautifully made and it served me at sea for forty-five years. I never changed it and never felt the need to buy a new one. In the middle of the ocean, say in the South Pacific where there wasn't a lot of traffic about, you were on your own. You were thousands of miles from any land and that was where your sextant came into its own. The only way you had of locating your position was using your sextant to observe the heavenly bodies and the various calculations to arrive at your position but at night, a nice calm night, say in the South Pacific, a full moon up there shining, it used to be absolutely beautiful.

The ships then needed a man at the wheel to steer them. Your watches were four on and four off and the watch from midnight to four in the morning was referred to as the graveyard watch and many a time when I was doing my two-hour stint at the wheel your eyes would shut and you would doze off. One moonlight night, the moon was more or less ahead of us. When I woke up the moon was right behind us. The ship had taken a round turn out of itself. Anyway, we were out in the middle of nowhere. There was no traffic. You could do what you liked more or less. It was unbelievable you know and the silence. The only thing you heard was a bit of a puff from the engine but the rest was absolute silence. You know on a calm night you could nearly pick the stars out of the sky with your hand, that kind of feeling you know.

You used to see the dolphins swimming alongside and the water was more or less, in lots of places, phosphorescent. They used to leave trails behind them and they used to frolic in the bow wash of the ship. You used to see maybe twenty or thirty of them leaping out of the water and having a great time for themselves and easily keeping up with the speed of the ship.

SEXTANT DEPENDENT FOR ACCURATE POSITION

I think of the times when I really needed the sextant when you were in some part of the world surrounded by reefs, little old coral islands, there is no lights or markings on them. At night-time you had to be very, very careful indeed. You depended on your sextant then to give you an accurate position.

Never in my life did I lose my sextant. I never mislaid it. When I was travelling with it, it was never part of my luggage. I carried it with me when I was travelling on trains or if I was flying up aloft, there it was always with me in the seat I was in. It never left my side. It was a very personal thing. I suppose you became attached to it. You realised the value it had to you. It probably saved my life on more than one occasion. At times I miss the tranquillity of it but when I retired I felt I had had enough of the sea and I never had any great desire to go back to sea. Fortunately, I was married to a very understanding woman and we got on very well together. So, I suppose, that was the reason why I did not want to go back.

The sextant is still in my bedroom and now and again I take it out of its case and I go through the motions of taking observations of the heavenly bodies and just put it back again.

LATITUDE AND LONGITUDE

To try and explain about latitude and longitude at sea when we used to use the sextant to navigate.

Latitude is north and south that is your position between the pole and the equator both north and south and latitude can be ascertained quite easily, it usually is through observations of the sun.

Now longitude is a different kettle of fish and it depends entirely on Greenwich Mean Time to the second. It makes a big difference when you take an observation of the sun or any heavenly body, if your time is not correct and it is essential that your chronometer is kept up to date and looked after.

Longitude is your distance on the equator or north or south of the equator or any position on the globe but it has got to be east or west of the prime meridian of Greenwich and when you take your observation you must have the exact time at Greenwich when you take it, otherwise your observation will be quite a bit in error. Longitude, again, is from east to west or west to east and it depends on exact time. So, it is rather difficult to try to explain to a person that hasn't any knowledge of navigation at sea but this is the best I can do. I will leave it at that.

A HOT TRIP

I spent several years on the New Westminster City as Master. My first trip was from Rotterdam to Dakar to load phosphate for Japan. We discharged at Muji. From there across to Portland, Oregon and loaded grain to Hamburg. Time chartered at Hamburg to a German firm to load general cargo for the Persian Gulf and the Red Sea ports, loading at Antwerp, Rotterdam, Marseilles and Genoa. We went through the Canal and commenced our first discharge at Nassau. Then on to Aden, Dubai and Kuwait and Basra, Khorramshahr, Abadan, Asab. That was a hot trip. Red Sea and Persian Gulf are not my favourite places.

Whilst I was up to the Persian Gulf I picked up a few pre 1914 gold sovereigns and got them at very good prices. Years later when the price of gold was sky high I managed to get quite a good price for them. I also got my good lady wife some decent gold bracelets up there, twenty-four carat stuff. Quite heavy ones, which she still has. My local Agent put me on to that business. He knew his way around and so I was in good hands.

ON THE END OF A PARACHUTE

After leaving the Gulf we came down to Bombay and loaded iron ore for Japan. We discharged there and again time chartered by the Japs, general cargo for the west and east coast of the U.S.A. New York was one of our discharge ports. I called in and saw my relatives there. Old Uncle Pat. Eugene and his wife. I had dinner with them several times. In fact, I had dinner with Eugene in his place where he had his medical office. That was in the Chrysler Building in New York.

BANISHED FROM WEXFORD TO THE USA WHEN PREGNANT

I also saw my mother's relatives over in Brooklyn. My mother's sister, Aunt Katie, in her young days in Wexford had the misfortune to become pregnant out of wedlock. That was one of the deadly sins in those days. She was literally banished from her home and she had to go all the way to the U.S.A. because whatever would the neighbours say when the truth came out? The people who banished her were all good Catholics, as the saying goes, eating the Stations off the wall.

Anyway, she went to the States. I am not sure how she got there because I did not know too much about her at the time and nobody else wanted to know about her. Nobody wrote to her for years. Talk about good Christians ye Gods! Where was the Christian charity of her nearest and dearest? It was only in the latter years that their conscience pricked them and they started to correspond again.

My Aunt Katie had said, "Mark will end up one day in New York and he will surely come and see me." I had been in the States quite a few times and would end up in New York. Well, she was quite right but I had left it too late. When I arrived at her house it was her daughter who greeted me saying, "My mother's words have come true when she said one day you would surely come and see her." I stayed a few days with her husband, daughter and met other cousins. She was a very nice person. She showed me all around the place. I thoroughly enjoyed it. I often think about my Aunt Katie. What she had to go through to be banished from her home just because she got herself pregnant. Sad isn't it?

CONEY ISLAND 600 FEET PARACHUTE DROP

I was given a good time. It was the only occasion when I had the experience of what it is like to be swinging on the end of a parachute. Coney Island in those days was the Disneyland set up for New York. We all went down there with my mother's relations.

One of the amusements down there was a 600 feet open tower with outriggers. Having imbibed well, but not wisely, I was persuaded to have a go on this tower. Over my head was a parachute. I was hoisted to the top, 600 feet up. Bloody hell I never sobered up so quick in all my life. The higher and higher I got looking down at the people as they got smaller and smaller. Eventually I reached the top and the parachute was automatically released and yours truly dropped about 100 feet before the parachute fully opened and slowed me down.

The remainder of the trip down was quite pleasant, after I got my heart and other parts of my anatomy back in their proper places. The parachute was, of course, guided down on wires so there was no drifting about and when you hit the bottom you landed on a trampoline set up. It was an experience I never wanted to repeat believe me.

A BOOZY CROWD

When we eventually sailed from New York we passed quite close to Coney Island and the above contraption. I said to the Mate, who was on the bridge with me at the time, that I had jumped from the top of that thing. He didn't believe me. I can't say I blame him very much. Not the kind of escapade you expect the Old Man of the ship to be up to, especially when he is always going around preaching about being careful and don't be doing anything stupid and all this kind of stuff.

There was I jumping off bloody towers 600 feet high. I suppose you do stupid things once or twice in your life. You can't be cute all the while and, as I say, those relations of mine in Brooklyn were quite a boozy crowd. They were the direct opposite of Uncle Pat's family. That is father's people over in New York. They didn't drink whatsoever. In fact the Uncle Pat was pretty anti everything. I'll tell you a little bit of a story about that just now.

WHISKY ON THE ROCKS

When I was serving my time one of the ships I was on came into Philadelphia and I applied for leave. They gave me three or four days off. I went by

Greyhound bus from Philadelphia up to Newark, New Jersey. That was where my father's sister Essie lived at the time. I stayed with them and I had a very nice time. The old Aunt Essie was very nice but she was a teetotaller. She didn't smoke and was very inclined to be straight-laced, you know. In those days I was a young fella. I used to like to take a drink and hell around a bit. But there was no doing it there. Anyway, a friend of my father's, a lady friend actually that he had known before she emigrated to the States, invited me over to her place. She was a jolly soul. Her husband was quite a nice fellow. Of course, the great drink in those days used to be whisky on the rocks and I had a lot of whisky on the rocks.

A DIM VIEW OF ME

As soon as I was finished with those people I was to go and visit the Uncle Pat, who also lived in Newark in those days. Those people drove me up there and by the time I got there I was feeling the whisky I'd drank and my head was beginning to turn around a bit. Anyway, I went in there and met the Uncle Pat and his wife. His wife was a particularly nice woman. I was very fond of her actually. They were vegetarians. There was no red meat eaten in that house. I was there for dinner. There was a vegetarian meal put down in front of me. I am not quite sure what I got but (chuckle) halfway through the meal the mixture of the vegetarian food and the whisky I had didn't gel to well. The next thing I was up from the table and trying to get out through the back.

Now the American houses all have wire mesh all around the verandas. Just to keep out the insects, mosquitoes and things. I was trying to open this ruddy door and the wire mesh when everything I had eaten and drunk came up and I spewed it all over the bloody wire mesh. Oh God, I could see my Uncle Pat's face. I think he took a dim view of me then. I do not think he ever got over it. He was horrified.

YOU WILL NEVER GET THE IRISH OUT OF YOU

At that time his son Gene was away somewhere. I think he was in the Hopkins University or the Hopkins Hospital. He was studying to be a Doctor then. I was invited to stay the night with the Uncle Pat and the room I was to sleep in was Gene's room. Well that was fine. I made no objection to that. We had a very pleasant evening after I recovered from my debacle of spewing all over his (laughter) wire netting.

It came time to go to bed. This was the first time I had seen the room I was going to sleep in. I was shown into the room. When I went in the next flipping thing I saw on the table by the side of the bed was a human skull. Apparently, this was one of Gene's models. It wasn't a model it was a real skull. He used it in his medical studies. Well, it didn't go down too well with me. I said to his mother, "Either that skull leaves this room or I leave it because I am not going to sleep with a ruddy skull looking at me all night." She laughed and in the end she took it away. She said, "You will never get the Irish out of you." I said, "I don't suppose I will." Anyway, I went to bed and had a fairly good sleep (laugh).

UNCLE PAT THE OLDEST VETERAN IN NEW YORK STATE

Eighteen and came across to New York on a sailing ship to look for work. There was no work to be found in New York so he took another sail ship, which took him around Cape Horn. He eventually landed in San Francisco. Now that was a voyage. I think I remember him telling me that it took him nearly four months to do. When he got to San Francisco there was no work available there either in that part of the world so he took a job in the American Navy. A job he referred to as a writer. I suppose it was an American rank of some description. Anyway, he was in the American Navy in Manila when the Yanks liberated the Philippines from the Spanish. While he was there some Spanish battleship was sunk off the Philippines.

In later years when he retired there was a time when he was the oldest veteran in New York State. I believe every year when they had their veterans parade he used to be the guest of honour. He didn't march down Broadway. I believe he was driven down Broadway in his older days. He was quite a character. He did well for himself in the States. He worked all his life for the American Post Office. He rose to a fairly executive position in that outfit. He apparently had plenty of money when he finally retired. He lived to quite a good old age. He was well over ninety before he kicked the bucket.

My sister Maureen was over in New York for a holiday once. I think Gene paid her way over and gave her a very nice time. While she was there she said the Uncle Pat took her all over the place. She said he was faster on his feet and more agile than she was. She said he took her up to places like the top of the Empire State Building and through the war museums and other museums. All she wanted to do was get into the shops but Uncle Pat had no time for the shops. She said she could have well done without the museums if she could have got into the shops.

He was quite a man to say the least. I asked him why he never went back to Ireland. He said, "Well I'll tell you the reason why. If I went back now I would expect to find it as I left it. I would expect to be able to see people over there when I left and I know that is not possible. When I left it things were pretty tough. My memories of it are not all that good." He was quite honest about it. He said, "I never had any ambition to go back." Strangely enough his son Gene was the same. He never wanted to go back to Ireland. You know when you think of it, one half of the Yanks are touring around Europe and around Ireland looking for their ancestors but, as I say, the Higgins family over in the U.S.A. were not so inclined to do that.

PORTLAND MAINE STEVEDORES SPEAKING IRISH

We went up to Portland, Maine after leaving New York. We loaded a cargo of grain for Liverpool actually. Portland, Maine is quite a nice place. One peculiarity about that place was the stevedores that were actually loading the ship. The fellows that were trimming the grain into our lower holes and all the rest of it.

I happened to be down on the deck and lo and behold they were speaking in Irish. It seemed there was a small community living in or about Portland, Maine who I believe their forebearers emigrated from the west of Ireland many years ago. The bunch I spoke to were all Americans. Some of them had been back to Ireland but they certainly were not born in Ireland. They still spoke the Irish amongst themselves. Of course, they spoke English too. It is surprising how a language can survive isn't it? I believe there is a Welsh community down in Tierra Del Fuego in South America who still speak Welsh and speak nothing else but Welsh. They are a farming community. They live down there and retained their Welsh language. It is amazing isn't it?

POOR OLD FATHER DIED

I left the New Westminster City and was at home at the time the poor old father died. Babe and myself just made it over in time for the funeral. I remember we picked up Ray in Dublin. I phoned him to say I was coming across. I had ordered a self-drive car from Ryans of Dublin to meet the ship. When the ship got into Dublin, Ray was there to meet me. We drove the car down to Wexford. As I said we just managed to get there in time for the Requiem Mass. It was then I heard that Gemmy's wife had suddenly died. Also Gemmy himself had died a few weeks previously. It was quite a traumatic time for the family with all the deaths, especially the poor old father. We saw him over to Crosstown and that was the end of him. God be good to him. He wasn't a bad chap at all.

I stayed at home in Wexford with Muds for several days.

Then Babe and I took off in the hired car and went across to Connemara. Went up the West Coast and did a little bit of touring around there. We went to Achill and a few other laces. It was a beautiful September. It was really very good weather. It was cold and frosty but brilliant sunshine. One of those nice Indian summers.

Under the circumstances we enjoyed the few days we had together on the West Coast.

We eventually got back to Dublin with the car. What a bloody problem I had trying to get the car back to Ryans' Office. They had an Office out of one of the side Streets off O'Connell Street. I arrived in O'Connell Street but couldn't drive down there. It was a one-way Street. I went around several times. Down one side of O'Connell Street and up the next. In the end I pulled into the side, just where Ryans had their Office and waited there until a Garda came up to me and wanted to know why I was parked. I explained to him, "Look, I am trying to get down to Ryans' Office to hand this car back. I can't turn down that way. It's a one-way Street." He says, "Don't worry about it. Come on I will direct you down." Sure enough he took me down the one-way Street and said (chuckle), "There you are now your troubles are over." Babe and I laughed about that. It could only happen in Ireland. Anyway we got the car back safely and eventually got down to the ferry and made our way home again.

One story I omitted to tell you about my voyage on the New Westminster City. We were chartered by South African Marine. They were a State Firm actually government run. Reardon Smith had a lot to do with the organisation and the setting up of the shipping business for the South African Government. We were their main European Agents so we had a lot to do with them. Well, they chartered out the New Westminster City and I loaded general cargo around the North European Ports. Before we left Europe we picked up a passenger to take down with us. He was doing the round voyage, coming down to South Africa and coming back with us, as we were again time chartered by SAF Marine to load general cargo on the South African coast back to the U.K. and European Ports.

ACROSS THE BISCAY HEAVY WEATHER IN THE BAY

This was quite an interesting trip. On the way down to South Africa part of our deck cargo consisted of prize cattle. We had several very, very, expensive bulls on deck and quite a few high-class heifers. We even had to carry a special cattle man to look after them.

Well, after leaving our final European port we were on our way across the Biscay and we ran into very heavy weather in the Bay. Our ship caught a lot of heavy water on the fore deck and smashed up the pens that all these prize cattle were in. It was a ticklish situation whether the prize cattle went over the side or not, amongst other deck cargo. I managed to get her hove to and we rode it out. But the Mate and his gang and this cattle fellow were down there up to their necks in bloody water trying to resecure the cattle pens.

Meanwhile, all the prize bulls and heifers were going bloody mad, kicking all before them. One or two of our fellows were rather badly bashed in by the bloody bulls. It wasn't funny to say the least. Anyway, we eventually got it under control and we resumed our voyage when the weather abated. We finally got shut of the buggers in Cape Town. From then on it was quite pleasant.

We went around Port Elizabeth, East London, Durban, L.M. up as far as Beira. We discharged all our European cargo and started to reload again. We started at Beira, retraced our steps.

Did the same ports again and finally got into Cape Town to top up with cargo.

BOMBER HARRIS

In Cape Town I had another two passengers foisted on me. I don't know whether you would know of them but it was the famous Bomber Harris and his wife. They were making the trip back to London with me. Bomber Harris, due to his organisational skills, had been called by SAF Marine to organise the new Shipping Firm. He had done this and that was his job over.

He was going back to his home outside London. He even had his bloody car with him. That was three passengers I had now. Harris, his wife and this guy who was doing the round voyage.

I had to do a bit of entertaining so I had them into my room before dinner of an evening and they had cocktails or whatever they wanted to have and it was quite pleasant. Old Harris used to return the compliment. He would have me into his accommodation.

He was in the owner's suite. I got quite friendly with him in the end. I was very interested in him because, as you know, Harris was the Bomber Command supremo in the last world war. He was ordered to bomb Dresden but was criticised for bombing so heavily. It was an Allied bombing. It only became a big deal in retrospect.

I will say I was at home when the first thousand bomber raid actually took off from the U.K. Whatever part of Germany they attacked they laid waste. Up to then England had been more or less on the receiving end of it and morale wasn't all that bloody high.

Believe me, when this big raid was publicised it didn't half put the morale of the people up. It really was the start of the end of the Germans because he continued this. He was a pretty ruthless guy. He went after military targets but he also bombed Cologne, which didn't have a lot of military hardware around I believe. He destroyed a hell of a lot of beautiful buildings, you know, the usual. He did precisely what the Germans did to the British. They had bombed London and they bombed other cities like Coventry and, of course, Liverpool. They weren't too fussy about where their bombs landed, so it was a case of getting your own back I suppose.

After the war, I remember, Harris didn't go down too well. He never really got the honours that the other Commanders and some of the big naval fellows got. Bomber Command crews were denied a separate campaign medal and in protest at this establishment snub to his men he refused a peerage in 1946. He was the sole commander in Chief not to become a Peer. After the war he was awarded the American Legion of Merit and many other awards.

I got to know him very well and we used to have long conversations. I used to ask him about all this business during the war and how you could manage to organise thousand bomber raids. And you know when he told me what was involved it was really bloody fascinating. He said, "The Germans shot down quite a few of our planes but we lost more to collisions and the take offs and all the rest of it that we ever lost due to actual enemy action but you had to allow for that. You couldn't get a thousand planes up into the air without one or two of them banging into one another. He was very interesting. He was quite an old man then. He was over ninety when he died but he told me quite a few stories.

He said he had differences of opinion with Churchill. He was a rough guy. Now having said that he admitted that Churchill was the man for the job. He said, "I don't think there could have been another fellow that could have seen England out of the mess they were in except Churchill but, believe me, Churchill had his faults too." In 1953, Churchill insisted Harris accept a baroncy.

Lady Harris was a very pleasant lady. She used to smoke cigars but they were gentle looking cigars. One thing I thank her for is that she introduced me to Magi sauce which she had brought on board. I have enjoyed it ever since on my favourite lamb steaks. She was getting on then, of course, but she must have been quite a looker in her day. We eventually reached London and our passengers left us. I must say for Harris, before he left, he came up to my room and said, "Captain I am going now and have just come up to thank you very much for a very, very pleasant voyage. It was most relaxing. I enjoyed the company and I enjoyed your hospitality and I enjoyed the conversation too. Now you and your good wife must come and visit us at Goring when you are between voyages when you leave the ship." I said, "Yes we probably would." I never did you know, because, well I used to say, "What's the point? We had nothing in common apart from war time experiences but I was sorry to hear the old fellow died. He was quite a man.

NEW ORLEANS

We arrived in New Orleans and carried on up the Mississippi to Baton Rouge and loaded soybeans and grain. It took us some time to load as the cargo had to be separated. It gave me a chance to see some of the deep south. One was called the Andrew Jackson, which was at some time during the American Civil War, the headquarters of the Army of the South-the Confederate Army. I believe old Andy Jackson actually used the place. I remember there were some very good restaurants. The food in that part of the world was, to say the least, exotic. Just like Me Ma's! God be good to her.

We sailed from Baton Rouge and came down the Mississippi. When you think of it that is a mighty big river you know. It took us ten hours to sail down from Baton Rouge to the mouth of the river where we discharged our pilot. I think we were drawing about five feet of water and there were no problems. We had plenty of water all the way to Baton Rouge. We dropped the pilot at the entrance and set off for the Panama Canal. We went through the Panama Canal and then we had the long haul to Japan. I think it took us twenty-seven days. It was mainly fine weather, clear sunny skies and generally calm seas. The only land we sighted on route was the Hawaiian Islands. We used to love those long sea passages. Life used to be very peaceful. No telephones to answer and the only contact we had with the Head Office was to let them know my position every five days and our ETA at the next port of call and that was on cable. So, I was a completely free agent.

YOKOHAMA

We arrived at Yokohama and tied up on the buoys there to discharge into lighters - part cargo. I went ashore and cleared the ship and while I was returning from the Agents to the dockside the taxi in which I was travelling in was involved in a crash with a ruddy truck. I ended up in the front seat with the driver. I was shaken but reasonably intact. The cab was a write off. (Now you know why I used to love the long sea passages). I went to hospital for an examination. No bones broken and no serious damage. Only bruises. It was the fault of the poor old cab driver and he was fired. The taxi firm were good to me because I did not sue them. They gave me lots of presents, one of which was a very sophisticated tape recorder that I still have.

Whilst in Yokohama I met up with the Mate of the Australian City. We saw quite a lot of each other. He had several meals with me on board and I with him on their ship. I knew the Skipper a fella by the name of Captain Harvey. He came from Belfast. We had lots of trips ashore and it was quite enjoyable. Japan in those days was still quite good. The pound still went a long way. Prices in Japan were very reasonable in those days. I know in my later days in Japan it was more expensive than the U.SA. The prices of everything had gone sky high. We hear a lot about the Japanese domination of the commercial world but the people of Japan themselves do not seem to have benefitted. Well, at least, the vast majority in many ways do not seem to have benefitted by all their prosperity.

MEALS

When my good wife died. I learnt to cook. I was not too bad at a roast dinner. Regarding curries, I had very good teachers. I had Indian crew who taught me. I would cook a batch and freeze some and other meals like casserole steak. I enjoyed what I made. I did not like fowl. My favourite always was a lamb steak with Bomber Harris's wife's recommended Magi sauce.

I liked woodwork. Working with wood gives great satisfaction. I enjoyed the things I made; little tables, bird boxes etc. I also got great satisfaction from my flowers. I was rewarded. You should embrace flowers. Put your arms around trees and embrace them.

NURSING HOME

After living with my daughter and son in law a few years I am now in a Nursing Home.

The staff are kind. I enjoy my food. I am confined to a chair. I have not the use of my limbs. At the moment, I am in acute pain as I have fractured my arm and my legs are shaky and painful. When you are feeling bad you should look bad. You would get a lot more sympathy.

22nd AUGUST 2021

When asked, "Are you happy?" His reply, "Oh yes, jumping over the moon," laughing.

"The word is content. Resigned. I have lived a long life and I realise you come to the end of it. I have come to the end of mine. I might as well be dead. Except for yourself and Babs I have no interest now whatsoever in life and that is a good way to be. Nothing interests me. It is time I was on the other side having a cup of tea with the Good Lord."

Mark went for his cup of tea with the Good Lord on 31st October 2021.

Terry Hall, Mark's nephew also recorded Mark 's life story.

He has gone to his heavenly reward.

Printed in Great Britain
by Amazon

26870084R00106